Celebrating 40 years of Vatican II

CONTINUING
THE JOURNEY

Celebrating 40 years
of Vatican II

CONTINUING
THE JOURNEY

Bill Huebsch
General Editor

ThomasMore®
– *An RCL Company* –
Allen, Texas

Acknowledgment
The Scripture quotations contained herein are from the New Revised
Standard Version Bible: Catholic Edition copyright © 1993 and 1989 by the
Division of Christian Education for the National Council of the Churches of
Christ in the U.S.A. Used by permission. All rights reserved.

Send all inquiries to:
Thomas More® Publishing
An RCL Company
200 East Bethany Drive
Allen, Texas 75002-3804

Telephone: 800-264-0368 / 972-390-6300
Fax: 800-688-8356 / 972-390-6560

Visit us at: **www.thomasmore.com**
Customer Service E-mail: **cservice@rcl-enterprises.com**

Printed in the United States of America

Library of Congress Control Number: 2002108998

7494   ISBN 0-88347-494-8

1 2 3 4 5   06 05 04 03 02

Dedication

To Dick Leach
for his commitment
to the vision and energy
of the Second Vatican Council.

Contents

Introduction

I SUPPOSE YOU COULD SAY THAT THE "JOURNEY" which this book addresses began the moment the followers of Jesus left their hiding places and allowed the Holy Spirit at Pentecost to lead them to the ends of the world. Ever since then, we Christians have been working to understand more deeply the unfathomable heart and word of God. We've been on a rather long journey. We've been holding meetings—called Sunday Assemblies—every single week since those earliest years, gathering to worship, but also to hear the Word broken open and made more able to penetrate our lives.

Down through the years, there has been another "word" which we have also gathered to consider. You might call it "the word of the church." That is precisely what it is. Because over the centuries we church people have been holding other meetings, outside of but closely related to those Sunday assemblies. At these other meetings, we've added one statement after another to a sort of twenty-centuries-long midrash on God's Word. In council after council, the church has gathered, both regionally and universally. Statement after statement, official pronouncement after official pronouncement, encyclical after encyclical, synod after synod, parish pastoral council meeting after parish pastoral council meeting—down through the centuries—a long series of meetings, all intended to help us women and men understand, live, and worship more fully by the light of the Gospel. Vatican II added a large, modern voice to this collective word, to this midrash. Not only is this "word" found in the official council documents themselves but also in the way they were written, the method of debate, the charity of the bishops, the reporting of the journalists, the speeches of the popes, and the ways in which the council was implemented around the world.

In the same way that Vatican II continued the journey begun at Pentecost when they came out of hiding and formed the church, this book offers eight essays that help continue the journey of which Vatican II is a part. These reflections will stimulate you, excite you, cause you to think more deeply about all this, and maybe even make you angry! Good! The purpose of this book is to help you jump into this ages-old conversation and add to it.

Nathan Mitchell from the University of Notre Dame leads this off with a prophetic statement about the need for poets and prophets in the church. (He is one himself, as you'll see when you read his essay.) Pope John was one of these, he tells us, but we can be, too. "Let us pray," he writes, "to become worthy of water and oil, of bread and wine. . . ." Poet and prophet, indeed.

Robert Kaiser who lived in Rome and covered the council for TIME Magazine, winds things up at the end of this book by calling on everyone to speak up, "for God's sake!" "You can give voice to what you want to see the church—your church—become. This is a prophetic act," he writes.

In between these two, Maureen Sullivan calls us all back to hope, and to the heart of our faith, Jesus Christ and the Holy Spirit. One can't read this essay without agreeing with her that ". . . with the Holy Spirit there are moments when the impossible becomes possible, moments when the unthinkable becomes thinkable." After reading this essay, you'll want to run out and shout that to the mountaintops!

Then Timothy Mullner steps forward to retell the story of the council itself—indeed, hope does seem possible when you read this story again! It is, he says, the greatest story NEVER told! This essay is filled with principles, which Mullner draws from the unfolding of the council itself, principles that will guide you now to continue this journey.

Monika Hellwig, echoing both Mitchell and Kaiser, lays it on the line in her usual frank style: whoever you are and however you got involved with Jesus Christ in your life, you are a prophet, so start acting like one! Prophets are ordinary, Hellwig reminds us. If you're reading her essay, you probably are called to be one. We must, she insists, get off the sidelines and into the game. The signs of our times all lead us to this powerful conclusion.

Maurice O'Connell steps up to the bat and continues the story with the voice of a pastor. Toward the end of his essay he asks: "Now honestly, aren't you sad to see that this article is coming to an end?" And indeed, every reader is sad to see his stories end. But as O'Connell suggests, go out and learn more about Vatican II yourself. There's a reading list at the back of this book. Use it as your guide and get started, he says.

My own essay is next. I provide you with an exploration of the method used by the council fathers to reach decisions and implement reform. Can this method be used today by all of us to address the vexing modern challenges facing us as the church? I hope so. And I try to spell this out by offering specific principles for reform, steps to follow to get there, and a list of items that were simply not on Vatican II's packed agenda, but which are before us today, some forty years later. Take these agenda items one by one to your pastoral council meetings; follow the principles and take the steps—see what happens next!

Jacquie Jambor then leads us down a very practical pathway through the sacraments. How could a collection of essays like this one not turn eventually to consider the sacraments? They're such a central part of every Catholic life. She provides a clear, concise treatment of the renewal and reform and reinvention of the sacraments of the church. No one could read this essay without wanting to roll up his or her sleeves and start responding to the challenges that Jambor names here. "Obviously," she points out, "the work begun at the Second Vatican Council is not yet completed."

At last, there's Bob Kaiser's frank assessment of the council, of the papacy of John Paul II, and of today's church. Playing a bit of mischief, he urges us to speak out about what hurts the church, and to celebrate all the hope we have among us.

WOW! THIS BOOK HAS THE POWER to change your life—or at least to change how you view today's church. Whether you were born well before, smack in the middle of, or long after Vatican II, this book offers you a way to jump into the dialogue begun in the church during those heady years. This book would make good "group reading," because one can't help but want to talk about all that's here with others who share this journey, too.

These eight writers were all participants in the thirtieth annual East Coast Conference held in Washington, D.C., in February, 2002. Hosted by Tim Ragan, this annual conference never fails to bring together great minds and ideas. Thomas More Publishing is grateful to Tim Ragan, and to these writers, for permission to publish the proceedings of that conference, albeit rewritten for this context.

—Bill Huebsch
Pine City, Minnesota

Contributors

Nathan Mitchell

NATHAN MITCHELL received his education at St. Meinrad College (B.A., Classics), Indiana University (M.A., Religious Studies), and the University of Notre Dame (Ph.D. Theology). He currently serves as Associate Director for Research at Notre Dame's Center for Pastoral Liturgy, where he is also editor of their publications, *Assembly* and *Liturgy Digest*. He has written several books on liturgy including *Real Presence: The Work of Eucharist* and *Mission and Ministry*. He also writes the "Amen Corner" for *Worship* magazine (Liturgical Press). In 1998 he received the Berakah Award from the North American Academy of Liturgy.

Maureen Sullivan

MAUREEN SULLIVAN, O.P. is a Dominican Sister of Hope from New York. She received her M.A. in Theology from Manhattan College in the Bronx and her Ph.D. in Theology from Fordham University. At present, she teaches theology at St. Anselm College in New Hampshire.

Timothy Mullner

TIMOTHY MULLNER brings over twenty years of parish and diocesan experience to his work as Executive Marketing Director at RCL in Dallas. Timothy holds a B.A. in Religious Studies/Youth Ministry from the College of St. Scholastica in Duluth, Minnesota, and an M.A. in Ministry and Spirituality from Seattle University. A frequent speaker at parish missions, conferences, and retreats, Timothy served as Program Director for RCL's Vatican II Center and he also taught on the adjunct faculty at St. John's University in Collegeville, Minnesota.

Monika Hellwig, LL.B., Ph.D

MONIKA HELLWIG, LL.B., Ph.D., is Executive Director of the Association of Catholic Colleges and Universities. She was formerly the Landegger Professor of Theology at Georgetown University where she taught for three decades. She has written and lectured extensively, nationally and internationally, both in scholarly and in popular contexts, in Catholic systematic theology and interfaith studies. She is a past president of the Catholic Theological Society of America. Her published books include: *Understanding Catholicism, The Eucharist and the Hunger of the World,* and *Guests of God: Stewards of Creation.*

Maurice O'Connell

MAURICE O'CONNELL is a priest of the Archdiocese of Washington, D.C. He has been a chaplain and teacher in a Catholic high school for eight years. He spent a year in South America preparing for ministry in the Hispanic community and was the pastor of a multicultural parish for ten years. He is now the pastor of a parish in Southern Maryland. He is coauthor of a high school text on church history entitled, *The Church Through History.*

Bill Huebsch

BILL HUEBSCH earned his B.A. in Religious Studies at the University of North Dakota and his Masters in Theological Studies from the Catholic Theological Union of Chicago. He serves as editorial advisor to the Benziger Publishing Company. He also worked for five years each on the diocesan staff in Crookston and New Ulm in Minnesota and as vice-president at RCL in Allen, Texas. In 1990 he established the Vatican II Project to promote the spirit and energy of Vatican II throughout the church. He has published a dozen books in recent years including three *Vatican II in Plain English* titles and most recently, *Whole Community Catechesis in Plain English.*

Jacquie Jambor

JACQUIE JAMBOR has an extensive background in cate-chetical ministry as a teacher, catechist, adult educator, and director of religious education. After more than twenty-five years in parish ministry, she is now with RCL in Dallas as their national series author, and she has published professional articles in the areas of religious education, family systems, and sacraments. Graduate studies in sacramental theology and family systems combined with her background in education provide Jacquie with a holistic approach to catechesis.

Robert Blair Kaiser

ROBERT BLAIR KAISER covered Vatican II for *TIME* magazine, worked on the religion beat for *The New York Times*, and served as journalism chair at the University of Nevada Reno. Two of his ten published books deal with Vatican II: *Pope, Council and World* and *The Politics of Sex and Religion*. Kaiser won the Overseas Press Club Award in 1963 for the "best magazine reporting of foreign affairs"—for his reporting on the Vatican Council. Editors at three news-papers have nominated him for Pulitzer Prizes. Since the fall of 1999, Kaiser has been a contributing editor in Rome for *Newsweek* magazine. Under contract with Alfred A. Knopf, he is also writing a book there on the future of the church.

Forty Years
Since Vatican II

ONE OF THE GREATEST PLEASURES OF GROWING
older arises when gratitude slowly fills the space in one's heart
that greed left behind. Aging, in fact, is that time in life when
one is challenged to surrender gracefully the possessions of
youth—but not its pride and never its passion. Passions—like
poems and prophecies—are, of course, incendiary. Like phos-
phorus, they can burst into flame at any moment, scattering
stars like sparks among stubble. The world—so poets and
prophets say—was made by the singer for the dreamer. Maybe
this is why the great Irish wit and raconteur Oscar Wilde once
wrote that the authorities are always willing to forgive a
criminal—but they're never ready to forgive a dreamer.

   Wilde's aphorism occurred to me recently as I was
reflecting on the life of Dorothy Day. She was born almost
one hundred five years ago (her birth date was November 8,
1897). Dorothy was, well, different—a dissenter, a doubter
who became deviously faithful to the gospel of justice and

peace. Dorothy Day was all those things the Christian Coalition (and its Catholic allies) loves to hate: A lively young woman with a keen intellect, a clear eye, and a sharp tongue. A loud, uppity critic. Part of a piquant, rowdy literary crowd. Addicted to love affairs. Unwed and pregnant. Suicidal, after an abortion.[1]

Later married to (and divorced from) a man twice her age. A Communist. A single mother raising her young daughter in Catholic Worker houses. A socialist ideologue. A protester. A passionate pacifist at a time (on the eve of World War II) when any woman who didn't aspire to be "Rosie the Riveter" seemed treacherous, and indeed treasonable. An ascetic who hated fasting. A pale, white-haired grandmother hauled off to prison for supporting Cesar Chavez in California.

A gutsy realist who claimed her besetting sins were gluttony and sloth—and who (while fasting with a small group of women in Rome during the final session of the Second Vatican Council) "made sure she had first filled her senses by going to the opera *(Cavalleria Rusticana)* before the fast [began]."[2] "I can't bear romantics," she once said. "I want religious realists. I want people who pray to see things as they are and do something about it."[3]

To hope and dream, yet to see things as they are—and to do something about them. Perhaps, in some quiet corner of your heart, you too heard that difficult, defiant prophet Dorothy Day calling out to you:

> Come to the living God,
>> Come to find, to meet, to hold
>>> the living, loving God
>>> made new for us in bread and wine.
>> Come to stand alongside the poor.
>> Come to struggle with those who seek freedom.
>> Come to resist all that offends God's justice.
> Come to the living God, the *disturbing* God.[4]

The living God. The disturbing God. The God who creates difficult saints, pushy prophets. The God who troubles the waters. I invite you to "celebrate the journey" and "face the continuing challenge" of an *aggiornamento* which began in our church forty years ago, in October of 1962.

Continuing the Journey: Why Vatican II Still Matters!

In his long poem "A Passage to India," America's "solitary singer," the poet Walt Whitman, wrote:

> After the seas are all cross'd (as they seem already cross'd,)
> After the great captains and engineers
>   have accomplish'd their work,
> After the noble inventors, after the scientists,
>   the chemist, the geologist, ethnologist,
> Finally [finally!] shall come the poet
>   worthy of that name,
> The true son of God shall come singing his songs.[5]

Finally shall come the poet. As Lutheran biblical scholar Walter Brueggemann has pointed out, we live in a "prose-flattened world," a world where the gospel is "a truth widely held, but a truth greatly reduced . . . a truth that has been flattened, trivialized . . . [T]he gospel is simply an old habit among us, neither valued nor questioned. But more than that, our technical way of thinking reduces mystery to problem, transforms assurance into certitude, revises quality into quantity, and so takes the categories of biblical faith and represents them in manageable shapes."[6]

Such a gospel contains no danger, no energy, no potency, no opening to newness. The result is distortion, stagnation. Instead of parabolically subverting our expectations, the gospel begins to look and sound like us. And when that happens, my friends, we know we're in trouble! Because the goal of Christian faith is not a gospel that looks like us, but a people who look like the gospel. As Andrew Greeley once said:

> The only real Jesus is one who is larger than life, one who escapes our categories, who eludes our attempts to reduce Him for our cause. Any Jesus who has been made to fit our formula ceases to be appealing precisely because He is no longer wondrous, mysterious, surprising. We may reduce Him to a right-wing Republican conservative or a gun-toting Marxist revolutionary and thus rationalize and justify our own political ideology. But having done so, we are dismayed to discover that whoever we have signed on as an ally is not Jesus. Categorize Jesus and He isn't Jesus anymore.[7]

Father Greeley is right on target. Jesus is precisely the one who fits no formulas, conforms to no categories. Such too are the conditions of discipleship. The mad nineteenth-century German philosopher Friedrich Nietzsche once wryly wrote that "Christianity came into existence in order to lighten the heart; but now it has to burden the heart first, in order to be able to lighten it afterward."[8]

In a word, Christianity aims to be a poem—but often it sounds like a pedantic sermon, a finger-wagging scold, a syllabus of errors. For centuries, Christianity has suffered from creeping certitude, from an obsession with "being right at all costs," from a compulsion to find clear and distinct ideas that will confound heretics and comfort the orthodox. But the gospels–those four, ancient "great poems" about Jesus–confront us with questions rather than clarity.[9] Their language is the memorable speech of poetry, of metaphor, of multiple meanings, of narrative ambiguity, of limitless potential. The gospels don't define, they describe. They don't define doctrine, they describe deeds, doubts, defiance, debates, decisions–and finally, a death.

In the introduction to his great work on theological aesthetics, Hans Urs von Balthasar wrote that "God needs prophets in order to make [the divine self] known, and all prophets are necessarily artists. *What a prophet has to say can never be said in prose.*"[10]

What a prophet has to say can never be said in prose. Friends, take notice. If we fail, it will be, in large part, *because we have bored people to death*—we've given them prose, when what they need is poetry. Postconciliar conservative critics might well disagree with me. "It's truth people need," they might argue. Fair enough—but truth held too close, too long, kills us. This is why we need the gutsy, in-your-face protests of a Dorothy Day, the bold vision of a Thea Bowman, the searing challenge of an Oscar Romero, gunned down as he celebrated eucharist with his people.

Prophets are those "necessary angels" among us, who shatter settled reality, who tell us the ball is in our court, who show us the divine in the daily, the holy in the homely, the sacred in the secular, the truth in the fiction. They remind us that the world is always ready to forgive the criminal–and execute the dreamer.

When Dorothy Day began her prophetic mission at *The Catholic Worker* in the early 1930s, she was one of a tiny group of women and men who formed what we then called "the lay apostolate." Laity were charged with the "dirty work" of carrying the gospel to a wicked world, while the "real" apostles—the clergy—got on with the more serious business of sanctifying sinners through the sacraments! By the time Dorothy Day died fifty years later (1987), lay ministers were a flourishing presence throughout the Catholic communities of North America, indispensable partners in the ministries of evangelization, catechesis, and liturgy.

In fact, if all the lay ministers in Catholic parishes in the United States were suddenly to go on strike some Sunday, parish life and worship as we know it would come to a screeching halt. Because, as Jim and Evelyn Whitehead pointed out more than fifteen years ago, we are a church that has finally come of age, a church that has returned from exile, a church that has recovered many of its ancient charisms, a church no longer afraid to dream, a church where "leadership" and "laity" are no longer mutually exclusive terms.[11]

OUR "COMING OF AGE," however, has come at a price; it's not exactly been a Sunday afternoon walk in the park. For much of the second millennium, lay people were resolutely exiled from any real roles of leadership in the church. The result was a church out of tune, out of touch, out of step, out of synch, out of luck, and just about out of time. And then— God sent us a prophet. Yes, she did! A short, playful, fat old guy with big ears and an even bigger grin. He laughed easily, and when he did, his whole body beamed—head, hands, and heart.

He was a seventy-eight-year-old "shuffling . . . voluble gourmand," who loved the Italian dialect and peasant food of his Bergamasque ancestors.[12] During World War II, he freely forged baptismal certificates so Jews could "pass" as Christians and thereby escape certain persecution and death.[13]

Finally came our poet, our prophet, and as you've probably guessed, his name was John, Angelo Giuseppe Roncalli—better known as John XXIII, *Blessed* John XXIII. The night before he was elected pope, Roncalli wrote in his diary: "Who is it that rules the church? Is it you or the Holy Spirit? Well, then, Angelo, go to sleep! I feel as if I'm an empty bag that the Holy Spirit unexpectedly fills with strength."

"I feel as if I'm an empty bag that the Holy Spirit unexpected fills with strength!" Who else but John XXIII could compare himself to an old bag lady, just hangin' around, ready and waiting for God's grace? Who else but John could say "In my life, I've always sought last place?"[14] Who else but John could be so irked by pontifical pomp and circumstance that he once blurted out in distress, "I'm dressed up like some Persian satrap!"[15]

Who else but John thought it was about time for God to give us a new Pentecost? Who else but John would simply go to God and demand one? Who else but John thought the church should be ready and willing to talk things over with the world–not as scolding teacher to unruly pupil, but as partner to partner in the work of God? Who else but John believed that the good are always the merry? Who else but John believed you can't take the church away from the people? Who else but John loved people more than power, loved rogues and rebels more than self-anointed saints? Who else but John could look the entitled, touchy, parasitical culture that was the Roman curia directly in the eye and say "*Ecco!* Things are gonna change?"

Who else but John could say, "Listen to everything, forget much, correct little."[16] On John's calendar, it was always, exuberantly, spring–time to throw open the windows, time to let that fresh air and shining sunlight stream in.

So, on the morning of January 20, 1959, less than three months after his election to the papacy, this chubby little old man with a cherub's smile and a big belly had a sudden inspiration, an inspiration that sprang up, he later recalled, "like a flower that blooms in an unexpected springtime. A word, solemn and binding, rose to our lips. Our voice expressed it for the first time–a council!"[17] The following Sunday, January 25, John broke the news to a group of seventeen cardinals: "Beloved sons and venerable brothers!" he said, "Trembling a little with emotion, . . . we pronounce before you the name and plan of a double endeavor: A Diocesan Synod for Rome, and an Ecumenical Council for the Universal Church." [18]

The reaction of those cardinals was–well, words like "apoplexy" and "fecal hemorrhage" come to mind! When one of the curial elders complained that it would be impossible to organize a council before 1963 at the very earliest, John replied, "Good, then we'll have it in 1962." And when somebody asked him why on earth he wanted to call an ecumenical council, John replied, "Why? Why, in order to make our journey to the Father . . . a little less sad."

And by golly, John got his way. On the morning of October 11, 1962, the eighty-one-year-old John, blessed pope and prophet, solemnly opened the Second Vatican Council. His first word was the Latin verb for joy: "*Gaudet mater ecclesia.*" *Gaudet!* "Mother Church rejoices!" *Rejoices!* Imagine that! (Incidentally, "joy" was also the Council's *last* word, at its final session in December of 1965, when it issued the *Pastoral Constitution on the Church in the Modern World* entitled *Gaudium et Spes,* "Joy and Hope.") If the prelates who heard John call a council in 1959 had a fecal hemorrhage, imagine what they had when they heard John say on October 11, 1962:

> In the daily exercise of our pastoral ministry—and much to our sorrow—we must sometimes listen to those who, consumed with zeal, have scant judgment or balance. To such ones the modern world is nothing but betrayal and ruin. They claim that this age is far worse than previous ages, and they rant on as if they had learned nothing at all from history–and yet, history is the great Teacher of Life. . . . We feel bound to disagree with these prophets of doom who are forever forecasting calamity–as though the world's

24

end were imminent. Today, rather, Providence is guiding us toward a new order of human relationships, which, thanks to human effort and yet far surpassing human hopes, will bring us to the realization of still higher and undreamed of expectations.[19]

PROVIDENCE IS GUIDING US toward a new order of human relationships! So said John—and how deeply we needed to hear those words; how deeply we still need to hear those words! One of my favorite books in the Hesburgh Library at the University of Notre Dame, where I work, is an oversize volume, about ten by fourteen inches, beautifully bound in scarlet watered-silk. On the front cover, stamped in gold leaf, are the Latin words *Concilium Oecumenicum Vaticanum II (Secundum)*, "The Second Vatican Ecumenical Council." The book was published in late 1962, just as the first of the Council's four sessions was ending. When you open that book, you discover page after page of photos, a veritable rogues' gallery of sclerotic-looking, superannuated cardinals and bishops, many of them older than God. You stare at these photos with astonishment, because you realize that these unlikely, stern-looking prelates were the very ones who, guided by God's Spirit, gave us *"Gaudium et Spes!"*

But as you know, of course, it took them a while! The first session of the council laid an egg, fired a blank–it produced no documents, no decrees, no dogmas, no definitions, no final decisions on pressing pastoral matters like evangelization, catechesis, or liturgical reform. The *Constitution on the Sacred Liturgy* had been debated, but no binding decision on its contents and future had been reached. When the first session of the council adjourned on December 8, 1962, the reviews were mixed and the results were inconclusive.

It wasn't until the *next* year, at the end of the council's second session (on December 4, 1963) that the liturgy constitution—entitled *Sacrosanctum Concilium*—was finally promulgated. By making liturgy its top priority the council had reclaimed one of the most ancient elements of our Catholic tradition, viz., that *we belong to the church by belonging to the church's worship*—an insight formulated by Saint Augustine and repeated 800 years later in the theology of Thomas Aquinas, who argued that baptism is the "*ianua sacramentorum*" which equips persons for participation in worship through the bestowal of "sacramental character." For Aquinas, baptismal character is not a "thing," not some "indelible mark," but a vital, permanent relationship that links individuals to the believing community conformed, through the Spirit, to the one priesthood of Christ.

None of this was easy. From time to time, curial conservatives and their allies attempted to hijack the council's proceedings and return to the "good ole days" when devout Catholics followed the old motto, "Pay, Pray, and Obey—and don't ask any questions!" By the early 1960s, after all, many of the church's senior cardinals were well into their dotage. One recalls the prefect of the Vatican Congregation of Seminaries and Universities, Giuseppe Cardinal Pizzardo (who was eighty-five when the council began).

Because of his prominent position, Pizzardo was often called upon to preside at eucharist in many of Rome's most important churches. But there was a problem. Like me, Pizzardo suffered from sometimes serious and frequent "senior moments" during which he would forget what came next in the ritual of the Mass. So his master of ceremonies had to function as a prompter.

"*Lege collectam, Eminenza,*" the MC would whisper. "Read the opening prayer, Your Eminence."

"*Lege evangelium, Eminenza,*" the MC would say. "Read the gospel, Your Eminence."

On one occasion, when Pizzardo had reached the fraction rite, the MC whispered *"Frange panem, Eminenza."* "Break the bread, Your Eminence." Nothing.

"Frange panem, Eminenza." Still nothing.

"Eminenza, tibi deprecor: frange panem." "I beg you, Eminence, break the bread!"

Pizzardo picked up the bread, gurgled something incomprehensible, and went CRRRUUNNCCH."

"Oh, Eminenza," the MC groaned, *"NON TOTALITER!"*

Yes indeed, only the Holy Spirit could have produced the Second Vatican Council. She knew what she was doing.

Cardinal Pizzardo's problems aside, the liturgy constitution was in fact a revolutionary document—not because it represented a "return to sources" but because it dramatically reinvented the liturgical act. To call what the council did for Catholic worship a "modest reform" or a mere "return to sources" is like calling the Big Bang a bonfire or a weenie roast that got a bit out of hand. The council didn't "renew," "retool," "return," "reform," "redesign," "refurbish," or "rehabilitate" the liturgy; it reinvented it. It radically democratized the liturgical act by insisting that "full, conscious, active participation" in worship is not merely "desirable" or "optional," but is "demanded *by the very nature of the liturgy itself*," as a baptismal right and obligation belonging to all.

The council insisted that the assembly is the subject—the agent—of the liturgical act, not its object. Going well beyond what Pope Pius XII had said fifteen years earlier in *Mediator Dei*, the council insisted that when the Eucharist is celebrated, the people "offer the Immaculate Victim" not only "through the hands of the priest but together with him."[20] True, each baptized person at the liturgy performs all and only those roles proper to their particular ministry—still, at the Lord's table, all the faithful "concelebrate," each in a distinctive but indispensable way.

ALL the baptized belong to the church by belonging to its worship. Fully. Consciously. Actively. So said Augustine. So said Aquinas. And so said Vatican II—and that is what made the council so revolutionary, so liberating. In a startling departure from what had been ecclesiastical "normalcy" for more than four centuries, the council decided to *trust* people. It decided to trust their customs and cultures, their insights and idiosyncracies, their baptismal dignity as "a chosen race, a royal priesthood, a holy nation, a redeemed people."[21]

It decided to trust the radical dignity of women and men, their radiant mystery.[22] It decided to trust the active (if often invisible) working of grace in the human heart, "for we must hold that the Holy Spirit offers to all the possibility of being made partners . . . in the paschal mystery."[23] It decided to trust all those "seekers after truth, persons of thought and science . . . explorers . . . of the universe and of history . . . pilgrims en route to the light."[24] It decided to trust the people who love beauty and who work for it, "artists, poets . . . painters, sculptors, architects, musicians, people devoted to the theater and the cinema." "If you are friends of art," the council said, "you are our friends."[25]

In short, the council didn't merely change the way we worship, it radically redefined the church. No longer could the church be identified with a small celibate cadre of religious professionals who sip espresso each morning, eat substantial quantities of pasta for lunch, and nap much of the afternoon. No longer could the church be confused with a good-old-boy network of curial careerists who make rules for others about marriage and sex, when their own ethics couldn't be detected with the aid of a particle accelerator. No longer could the church be confused with an essentially secular, shameless institution that grabs power, beats and berates its critics, and cannibalizes its best and brightest. As Joseph Cardinal Ratzinger said a few years ago at the Eucharistic Congress in

Bologna, Christians are meant to be a church of martyrs, not a church that makes martyrs.

Facing the Challenge:
A People Called to Prophecy
by Jesus the Prophet

I believe that Cardinal Ratzinger is right. But more importantly, I believe that John XXIII was right. It is springtime in the church, and though, as Robert Herrick said, "rough winds may shake the darling buds of May," I believe that John had it right when, as he lay dying, he told two Vatican diplomats, "Today more than ever, . . . we are called to serve [hu]mankind and not just Catholics, to defend above all and everywhere the rights of the human person and not just those of the Catholic Church. . . . [A] deeper understanding of doctrine [has] brought us to a new situation. . . . It is not that the Gospel has changed: it is that we have begun to understand it better." [26]

Looking at the crucifix near his bed, John said: "[That's] the secret of my ministry. . . . Those open arms have been the program of my pontificate: they mean that Christ died for all, for all. No one is excluded from his love, from his forgiveness." [27] *No one is excluded*, not even—well, in this post-September 11 world, I suspect you can fill in the blanks.

In short, John and the council proposed a new way for us to be church. The church is not a community of irreformable dogma, unquestioning obedience, and unconditional surrender; rather, as John reminded a group of Pax Christi delegates in 1961, the church is a community of peace whose members are willing "to walk along the road with *anyone* as far as possible." [28] Unlike modern American politicians who seem to confuse presidency with priesthood, John did not waste his time berating "the axis of evil;" instead, he proposed that both church and state replace denunciation with dialogue, closed minds with open doors. The church's future, both John and the council understood, is people—people like you.

It is surely no accident that *Lumen Gentium*, the Second Vatican Council's *Dogmatic Constitution on the Church*, begins by first speaking about the church as a "mystery," a "sacrament of unity" in and for the world,[29] a holy people whose premier manifestation is the celebrating assembly—one people gathered around one pastor at one altar/table. By appealing first to the church as mystery and "people of God," the council gave us not merely instruction and image, but a new theological hermeneutic. It said, in effect, that we must use "people of God" as the lens—the optic—through which we interpret every other aspect of church life, hierarchical, institutional, juridical.

In short "people of God" is the controlling metaphor that makes sense of all the others—including such ancient and venerable icons as Paul's "body of Christ." (Incidentally, for most of the first millennium, Catholic tradition understood the phrase "body of Christ"—without any qualifying adjective—as the people, the church; "the mystical body of Christ" referred to the eucharistic elements.)

So John and the council challenged us to become "people of God" first—disciples of Jesus, that disturbing prophet who was also, as the distinguished Catholic exegete Father John Meier says, a "marginal Jew," an insufferably ordinary "nobody" from "nowhere." Jesus wasn't afraid to live on the margins, at the edge of the raft—even though, as Father Meier points out, the margins were a scary place to be in a world where a privileged aristocracy of old-money families (the Sadducean elite of Jerusalem) controlled the Temple, its liturgy, its priesthood, its jobs, its markets, its income, its ideologies, and its public relations![30]

As a boy, Luke says,[31] He got lost. His parents panicked. Significantly, Luke does *not* go on to say that Jesus was rewarded with a scholarship to Jerusalem State University, where he earned an MBA in marketing, finance, or temple management—and was presumably given a BMW or a Mercedes at graduation. Rather, Luke says, Jesus returned to Galilee—to Galilee of the Gentiles, as it was sarcastically known. There, he eventually launched a ministry among the marginalized.

Long story short: Who knew? Who cared? In the eyes of most of his contemporaries, Jesus was a minor celebrity, a faint blip on the cosmic screen—a peripheral phenomenon, uninteresting and unimportant. His work was largely ignored by Jewish historians like Josephus and by Romans like Tacitus. To the Roman occupiers of first-century Palestine, Jesus' torture, trial and execution were simply the "ghastly death" that awaited any slave or rebel. To his coreligionists, Jesus' death on the wood of the cross was a certain sign that he had been cursed by God—for according to the Torah,[32] cursed is anyone hanged upon a tree.[33] But Jesus' marginalization didn't stop there. As John Meier writes:

> To a certain degree, Jesus . . . marginalized himself. At the age of roughly thirty, Jesus was an ordinary carpenter in an ordinary hill town of lower Galilee, enjoying at least the minimum of economic necessities and social respectability required for a decent life. For whatever reason, he abandoned his livelihood and hometown, became "jobless" and itinerant in order to undertake a prophetic ministry, and not surprisingly met with disbelief and rejection when he returned to his hometown to teach in the synagogue. In place of the "honor" he once enjoyed he was now exposed to "shame" in an honor/shame society, where the

esteem of others determined one's existence much more than it does today. Relying basically on the goodwill, support, and economic contributions of his followers, Jesus intentionally became marginal in the eyes of ordinary working Jews in Palestine, while remaining very much a Palestinian Jew himself.[34]

Jobless. Homeless. A vagrant. A grown man with no visible means of support. An unemployed, uninvited "house guest" who relied on the kindness of strangers. This is *not* a pretty picture. And it gets worse. Jesus lived—deliberately and voluntarily, it seems—outside the institutions of marriage, parenthood, and family. Indeed, Jesus *may* have been describing his own life choice in that violently offensive, shocking, and embarrassing metaphor found in Matthew 19:12: "Some are incapable of marriage because they were born so; some, because they were made so by others; some, because they have renounced marriage [the Greek says they have *eunuchized*, castrated, themselves] for the sake of the kingdom of heaven."[35] Tell *that* to Jerry Falwell and Pat Robertson!

Far from being a poster child for family values, Jesus' life was highly irregular and suspect. He rejected John the Baptist's program of asceticism—fasting, prayer, the harsh, abstinent life of the wilderness. He showed impatience (not to say outright hostility) toward his own family of origin.[36] He suggested that what really binds people into families is a shared spiritual vision, a faith, a way of living. Worse still, Jesus staunchly rejected a whole passel of patriarchal privileges—for example, the right claimed by Jewish *men* to divorce their wives (the men could often remarry; the women usually couldn't).[37]

But perhaps the greatest scandal of all was Jesus' status as a layman. John Meier puts it bluntly: He "was born a Jewish layman, conducted his ministry as a Jewish layman, and died a Jewish layman."[38] Like a Dorothy Day or a Mother Teresa or a Thea Bowman, Jesus did not belong to an entitled elite. He was, Meier eloquently writes:

> [A] no-account Galilean in conflict with Jerusalem aristocrats; . . . a poor peasant in conflict with the urban rich; . . . a charismatic wonderworker in conflict with priests very much concerned about preserving the central institutions of their religion and their smooth operation; . . . In short, that Jesus was a layman was not a neutral datum; it played a role in the development and denouement of his drama.[39]

Being a layperson was Jesus' ticket to certain failure in a world where the haves get more and the have-nots get had. What is more astounding still, Jesus embraced his failure, embraced it all the way to the cross. In life and in death, Jesus became what he healed. He didn't shout words of comfort at the leper from a safe distance; he touched the oozing sores and the rotting body parts—he became the leper's uncleanness.

At table in the house of Simon the Pharisee,[40] Jesus didn't push the weeping woman away or scrape her perfumed oil from his feet; instead, he opened his body to her tears, to her touch, to the luxuriant comfort of her hair—he became her brokenness, her repentance, her generosity, her love. And on the cross, Jesus became the death he died—he became the death of death, and thereby became the unutterable scandal of Easter and the empty tomb.

The implications of all this are truly terrifying. If the tomb is empty, we can meet the Risen Jesus only by seeking his presence in the poor, in the thick of life, in the least and littlest, in care and cult, in bread and wine, in a body gathered at table, in speech and song and sacrament. We have no choice but to become what the council called us: a Pilgrim People of God. Easier said than done, of course! For so long, as a church, we've relied on "the powers of the strong."

TODAY AND TOMORROW, we must learn to rely on the powers of the weak. We must move forward fearlessly—always with leadership, sometimes ahead of leadership, but never again "under" leadership. The "powers of the weak" is a phrase coined by social analyst Elizabeth Janeway. As Janeway points out, the problem with "the powers of the strong"—the problem with being in charge—is that you get used to it. Before long, you actually believe, with all your heart, that you are in charge—of everything, of everyone. And that is a dangerous place for a person to be. Jesus, you may recall, had something to say about such places and persons: "Woe to you. . . ."

I am not suggesting that we sentimentalize weakness. "Overall," as Elizabeth Janeway observes, "the weak are no more . . . warmhearted, Dickensian dears than women are by nature loving, nurturing, supportive adjuncts to husbands and bosses. Projecting such virtues onto those who do not hold power falsifies their real position."[41] The powers of the weak derive not from some Dickensian conflict between Ebenezer Scrooge and Tiny Tim, but from something far more basic.

We forget, often, that the powerful want something from the weak. And what they want isn't power (which they already possess in spades), but legitimacy—the right to power. Ironically, the weak have power over the one thing the mighty value most—namely, *the right to confer or withhold legitimacy.* "Disbelief," writes Elizabeth Janeway, "signals something that the powerful fear, and . . . we should not underestimate its force. It is, in fact, the first sign of the withdrawal of consent by the governed to the sanctioned authority of their governors, the first challenge to legitimacy."[42]

Our church leaders often remind us, of course, that the people of God are not a political entity, that the church is not a democracy. No kidding! But neither is it a totalitarian state based on an authoritarian regime of repression and thought control. The alternative to democracy is not, after all, Nazism or some other Fascist ideology. The alternative to democracy, for heaven's sake, is the gospel—Jesus' vision of a new human society based on the voluntary renunciation of hoarding, having, and controlling—those three addictions that divide and destroy us. Our species may not have learned much in the past million years or so, but one thing we have learned: "the governed" are not—and *were* not—mere "raw material to be 'manufactured' into a new order of being by obedience-training and behavior-modification."[43]

Today, we are called as church to exercise the powers of the weak. Jim and Evelyn Whitehead name four such powers: *the power to disbelieve* (i.e., the power to say "the way things are isn't the way things have to be"); *the power to join together* (i.e., the power to change social structures by overcoming isolation, by breaking the conspiracy of silence and secrecy); *the power to claim beliefs as our own*—not as something borrowed from or brokered by the powerful; and finally, *the power to act on what we believe.*

As we move further into the third millennium, we are called to be a church where power resides in the weak. We are called to become a church that doesn't dread dreaming; a church unafraid to become what it heals; a church that knows death is the path to life; a church that doesn't fear the body or its fluids or its failures; a church that knows the mysteries of matter reveal the mysteries of the spirit; a church that isn't afraid to fail; a church that isn't afraid to forgive—or to ask forgiveness; a church that isn't afraid of speaking truth to power.

As we move forward, let's dare to be a church that not only does eucharist but is eucharist. Let's dare to be a church in recovery. It doesn't take a rocket scientist to realize that for centuries our church has been in denial about many matters: about the Copernican revolution and the claims of science; about the consequences of its own terrible silence during the Holocaust; about women and their bodies; about the way married couples love each other and plan their families. In short, we have often been addicted, as a church, to lies, and half-truths, and silence at times when loud indignation and outrage are clearly called for.

As the French bishops wrote in their 1997 "Declaration of Repentance: "The time has come for the church to submit her own history, especially that of this [modern] period, to critical examination and to recognize without hesitation the sins committed by members of the church, and to beg forgiveness."[44]

A church called to recovery is a church bound to repentance. Let's be that church. Let's become that church. A repentant church in recovery is a church whose ego is deflated; a church *willing to pay the price* to find release from its bondage to self; a church able to renounce absolutism and control; a church eager to abandon the addictions of hoarding, holding, and having in favor of freedom, generosity, and the inescapable *insecurity* that always accompanies faith. A church in recovery is a church that knows the goal of Christian living isn't canonization, it's compassion—it's the capacity to feel fiercely, to love toughly, and to walk humbly with the God whose gift of self arrives always and only in the shocking company of strangers.

Some twenty-five years ago, my beloved teacher Aidan Kavanagh wrote these words:

The eucharist is a rite that intensifies change and causes it to take place continually according to that same pattern of Jesus' own change from death to a life no one had ever lived before. We break the bread of his body, we pour out the cup of his blood in sacrifice. Paul VI and Mrs. Murphy can know this: kings and paupers can know it: professors and freshmen can know it. It isn't hard . . . to know, but it is supremely difficult to live without sham or full-scale retreat. Baptism and eucharist are really one corporate person dying and rising. That is a lot to load onto simple things like water and oil, bread and wine. But they never complain. They have never sinned either. They are faithful and close to God in their original innocence, therefore, to a degree that staggers one's imagination. To become like them is what he came to show us. They are superb as God meant us to be. To get that way is a passion for us who have fallen, as it were, into reason.[45]

Let us pray to become worthy of water and oil, of bread and wine—elements innocent, faithful, close to God—superb as God meant us to be. Let us pray to become worthy of the poor, worthy of the people we serve. Let us remember always what the council said in its closing message to the poor:

All you who are poor and abandoned, you who weep, you who are persecuted for justice, you who are ignored, you the unknown victims of suffering: Take courage. . . . You are saving the world.[46]

1. See William D. Miller, *All is Grace: The Spirituality of Dorothy Day*. Garden City, NY: Doubleday, 1987, pp. 15–16.
2. *An Appetite for God*, p. 15.
3. Ibid.
4. Text [altered] by Jan Berry, in Janet Morley, ed., *Prayers for the Church Year*. Maryknoll, NY: Orbis Books, 1992, p. 9.
5. Section 5, lines 101–105.
6. *Finally Comes the Poet: Daring Speech for Proclamation*. Minneapolis: Fortress Press, 1989, pp. 1–2.
7. *The New York Times Book Review*, XCI:12, 1986, p. 3.
8. *Human, All Too Human: A Book for Free Spirits*, trans. Marion Faber, with Stephen Lehmann. Lincoln, NE: University of Nebraska Press, 1984, p. 87, aphorism 119.
9. See Oscar Wilde, *De Profundis*. Dover Thrift Editions; Mineola, NY: Dover Publications, 1996, p. 63.
10. *The Glory of the Lord: A Theological Aesthetics*. Volume 1: Seeing the Form; trans. Erasmo Leiva-Merikakis; ed. J. Fessio and J. Riches. New York: Crossroad/San Francisco: Ignatius Press, 1982, p. 43; emphasis added. Von Balthasar is quoting F. Medicus.
11. *The Emerging Laity: Returning Leadership to the Community of Faith*. New York: Doubleday, 1986. Chapter One, "The Community Comes of Age."
12. See Thomas Cahill, *Pope John XXIII. New York*: Viking/Penguin, 2002), p. 225.
13. See Lawrence Elliot, *I Will Be Called John: A Biography of Pope John XXIII*. New York: Dutton, 1973, pp. 166–167.
14. Henri Fesquet, *Wit and Wisdom of Good Pope John*, trans. Salvator Attanasio. New York: P.J. Kenedy & Sons, 1964, p. 36.
15. Fesquet, p. 44.
16. Fesquet, p. 85.
17. Elliot, pp. 287–288.
18. Elliot, p. 289.
19. Translation as in Cahill, *Pope John XXIII*, p. xiii.
20. *Constitution on the Liturgy*, 48.
21. See *Constitution on the Sacred Liturgy* 37; 14.
22. See *Gaudium et Spes*, 12–21.
23. *Gaudium et Spes*, 21.
24. Message to persons of science and thought at the close of Vatican II. *Council Daybook, Vatican II, Session 4*; ed. Floyd Anderson; Washington, DC: NCWC, 1966, p. 364.
25. Message to artists; ibid.
26. Cahill, pp. 211–12.
27. Ibid. p. 212.

28. Cahill, p. 194; emphasis added.
29. See *Sacrosanctum concilium*, 27.
30. John P. Meier, *A Marginal Jew: Rethinking the Historical Jesus.* Vol. 1: The Roots of the Problem and the Person. New York: Doubleday, 1991.
31. Luke 2:41–52.
32. Deuteronomy 21:23
33. Meier, p. 8.
34. Meier, p. 8.
35. *New American Bible* translation.
36. See Matthew 12:46–50.
37. On Jesus' views about divorce as they are presented in Matthew's gospel, see Douglas R. A. Hare, *Matthew—Interpretation: A Bible Commentary for Teaching and Preaching.* Louisville: John Knox Press, 1993, pp. 219–223.
38. Meier, p. 345.
39. Meier, p. 347; emphasis added.
40. Luke 7:36–49.
41. *Powers of the Weak.* New York: Knopf, 1980, p. 157.
42. Janeway, p. 162.
43. Janeway, p. 182.
44. September 30, 1997, (English translation in *Origins* 27:18 [October 16, 1997], 301–305; here 303.
45. "Initiation: Baptism and Confirmation," *Worship,* 46:3, 1972, pp. 262–276; here, p. 270.
46. See text in Walter M. Abbott, ed., *The Documents of Vatican II.* New York: Guild Press, 1966, p. 734.

I Hope You Dance

Introduction

"IF YOU HAD THE CHANCE, WHOM WOULD YOU like to interview?" Well-known talk show hosts like Larry King and Barbara Walters are frequently asked this question. Well, I am not a talk-show host. I am a Dominican Sister of Hope, a theologian, and a Roman Catholic. And I have a little confession to make—there is a chance that I might not be any of the above had it not been for the Second Vatican Council.

Of course, the initiator of that council was Pope John XXIII. He is the person I wish I had the chance to interview.

What would I say to him? For one thing, I would thank him for being "the manifestation of the Spirit in our time," as he has been called by one commentator.

I cannot imagine a greater tribute being given to any Christian. Each of us is invited to be just that—a presence of

God in the world—and yet most of us struggle throughout our entire lives to respond to this invitation.

This is why Angelo Roncalli, better known to us as "the good Pope John," deserves both admiration and emulation. It is why all of us involved in the process of passing on the Good News to a new generation must never forget the gift he *was* to the church or the gift he *gave* to the church—the Second Vatican Council.

And it's why I drew on a contemporary song for my title here: "I Hope You Dance."

Have We Lost the Momentum?

Many in the church today have either forgotten this remarkable moment in our history or—worse—simply don't know about it.

How could this be? So much has been written about the council. It has been called the decisive ecclesial event of this century. Never before in the history of Catholicism have so many and such sudden changes been legislated and implemented and immediately touched the lives of the faithful. And never before had such a radical adjustment of viewpoint been required of them.

It was the best prepared council in the history of the church and had representatives from every corner of the world—and not only Catholic representatives. Pope John also invited observers from the other Christian churches and religious traditions.

It was a moment of grace in the life of the church for so many reasons. Theologian Timothy McCarthy commented:

1. Instead of continuing a hostile and suspicious attitude toward the world, Vatican II asked us to live in close

union with our contemporaries, calling us to witness to the gospel in today's world.

2. Instead of regarding itself as spotless and all holy, the church acknowledged its errors, failings, and sins and saw the need to continually reform itself.

3. Instead of viewing the church primarily as a pyramid (with the pope at the top, followed by bishops, clergy, religious, and finally the laity)—it saw the need for all Catholics to work for the common good of the church and its mission, with no one in the church better than any other simply by virtue of one's vocation.

4. Instead of emphasizing that individual salvation is to be achieved in the next world—Vatican II called for the church to carry out its mission in this world and transform it by the grace of Christ.

5. Instead of viewing other Christian churches with hostility and other religions as false and harmful, the council called us to respect our brothers and sisters and—perhaps, in one of its greatest accomplishments—acknowledged that salvation is a gift that can be offered to all of humanity, not only Roman Catholics.

Yet Timothy Mullner refers to Vatican II as "the greatest story never told!" And Robert Blair Kaiser claims that our present pope has reversed Vatican II by a process of centralization and clericalism and by endorsing a kind of folk religion that has little to do with the Gospel of Jesus Christ and the vision of John XXIII.

In fairness, some of this is to be expected. As the great John Henry Newman once wrote: "It is rare for a council not to be followed by great confusion." And we do have a crisis in the church after the council on a number of levels.

Still, one of the great thinkers at the council, Dominican Father Yves Congar wrote: "I do not believe the present crisis in the church is the result of Vatican II." He claimed: "Vatican II was followed by sociocultural change more extensive, radical and rapid than any change at any other period in human history."

For those of us old enough to remember the 1960s, we recall a time of overall protest and disenchantment with authority at all levels. The church was not immune to this disenchantment.

In 1990, the church celebrated the twenty-fifth anniversary of the closing of the council. But it was a rather muted celebration. Yes, there were expressions of praise and gratitude for the many achievements of Vatican II. But several concerns were raised at the time and I note them here because these concerns remain valid even today.

The editors of *Commonweal* magazine, a Catholic journal, complained in 1990 that the strong resistance of the Roman Curia to the thrust of the council still survives and even enjoys the support of the pope. Archbishop Rembert Weakland of Milwaukee worried that the enthusiasm generated by Vatican II had spun itself out. He hoped the church would recapture the attitude that it is but a humble partner, an imperfect society, engaging this world in dialogue.

The view that Vatican II's momentum had diminished was shared by over four hundred theologians who in that same year endorsed a statement of the Catholic Theological Society of America accusing the Vatican of obstructing change in the church.

That statement, entitled "Do Not Extinguish the Spirit," claimed that the church's leadership had failed to implement the changes called for by the council in four particular areas of concern: collegiality of the bishops, cooperation between the magisterium and theologians, ecumenism, and the development of legitimate public roles for women in the church. Even a cursory reading of theological journals and newspapers today clearly demonstrates that these concerns are still very much with us.

I CONFESSED ABOVE that without the Second Vatican Council and the impact it had on every aspect of Christian living in the modern world, I wonder whether I would still be a Dominican Sister, a theologian, even a Roman Catholic.

Why do I think this? For one thing, I have had the advantage of living in "two churches"—the one before Vatican II and obviously in the renewed church after the council. I entered my congregation in August 1965, just three months before the council would end. And so I was able to observe religious life in a way that those who would come after me could not.

It was a time of transition for religious orders and, at times, a painful transition. Since I entered when I did, all of my training would be in the spirit and theology of Vatican II. *The Documents of Vatican II*, a compilation of all sixteen documents issued at the council, was one of my textbooks. I would soon be sent out to teach and live with other sisters who did not have the advantage I had. This produced the expected tension whenever two worldviews collide—and collide they did!

Before Vatican II's call for religious orders to renew themselves according to the spirit of their founders and in a manner that would put them in touch with the modern world, religious women understood themselves very differently. Obedience, humility, and docility were central virtues in the training of religious—not that those qualities are not good—it is just that they were carried to the extreme in many cases.

In addition, distortions crept into our understanding of these virtues. Obedience deteriorated into "blind" obedience and it was held that the voice of God could always be heard in the voice of the superior. It resulted in some very strange practices—perhaps you have heard the stereotypical story of the woman in training who was asked to water a stick, just to test her obedience.

Such an activity does test something, but I would not call it obedience!

Humility is another virtue that was much misunderstood. It began to look more like humiliation than the very real virtue it is. Perhaps you remember the movie *The Nun's Story* with Audrey Hepburn. She enters the convent in Belgium during World War II and has great difficulty adjusting. In one scene, she is told by one of her superiors that she should deliberately do poorly on a test to show her humility, to avoid the evil of human pride.

The virtue of docility also succumbed to misconceptions. Rather than produce women who were open to the teachings presented to them and willing to learn, more often than not we found women who could no longer think for themselves, who were frightened of authority and saw anything coming from an authority figure as ultimate truth.

Two personal stories might serve as examples. My first teaching assignment found me teaching forty-six first graders in the Bronx. One afternoon, I came home from school and told the superior I planned to visit the mother of one of my students that afternoon. She had had a baby.

My superior said: "We don't usually do that."

I honestly had no idea what she was talking about, so to add a little humor to the moment, I said: "What, have babies?'

Well, as you can imagine, she did not find me one bit humorous. I finally found out that she thought it would be inappropriate for me to visit a woman who just given birth—we have not had the healthiest attitude toward human sexuality over the years—but this is a topic for another time.

Another event comes to mind. I had the task of cleaning the dining room every week with another sister. She was an elderly woman and always appeared frail and nervous.

One day I suggested that perhaps we could skip one of the tasks—emptying, washing, and then refilling the salt and peppershakers. They weren't dirty. And I thought the time could be better spent doing something else.

She responded: "But Sister Mary Ann says we must do them every Wednesday." (Obviously, the name has been changed to protect the innocent!) Vatican II would bring many unexpected changes to the way religious life would be lived.

IN ADDITION TO BEING a Dominican Sister, I am also a theologian. Again, the council affected the role of theologians. Before the council, freedom of inquiry and dialogue on the part of theologians was frowned upon. In fact, a study of early twentieth-century church history gives us the names of many theologians who were silenced or in some way disciplined by the Vatican for attempting to dig deeper into the mystery we call God.

The theologian was seen as someone whose main task was to simply reiterate the teaching of the magisterium. The Second Vatican Council recognized that, as the pilgrim people of God, we are always moving toward the fullness of truth, who is God. And this pilgrimage requires that every generation study and probe more deeply the mysteries of the faith, trying to articulate the good news of Jesus Christ for another generation.

Dominican theologian Aidan Nichols defined theology as "the disciplined exploration of Revelation." Each of these words is important. Revelation is of course God's personal self-manifestation to us, and Nichols says that the theologian must consecrate himself or herself to the meaning of Revelation.

Theology is disciplined in the sense that theologians cannot say whatever they want—they are bound by the two sources of revelation, Scripture and Tradition. And, finally, it is truly an exploration, not simply a reiteration of past articulations. Theologians must constantly seek the deeper insights contained in the richness of revealed truth.

Theologians use the term "ongoing revelation" to describe the process. The truths themselves do not change, but humankind's understanding of these truths grows and develops in light of the new questions, data, and circumstances of each new generation.

The example of an onion helps explain this concept. Think of the truths of the faith present in the kernel of the onion. It becomes the task of each new generation of theologians to peel away the layers of the onion to receive the deeper insights.

John XXIII himself espoused this idea in his opening speech at the council when he stated: "The ancient deposit of the truths of the faith is one thing; the way it is articulated is another." Such an understanding makes it very exciting to be a theologian today—humbling too, because the object of our study is the infinite God who is best described as Mystery, a richness of meaning beyond the full comprehension of the human person

I AM ALSO A ROMAN CATHOLIC. But without the fresh air and integrity ushered in by Vatican II, I do not know whether I would be able to maintain that identity today. This is not to say that pre-Vatican II Catholicism was a bad thing. It was not. It produced many saints—some who are still among us.

But there is a basic principle that says for any organism to continue to live, it must grow and develop. John XXIII called for an *aggiornamento*, an updating, a renewal. And he called for a deepening of the faith.

Pope John saw a problem with the way we understood faith at the time. For reasons beyond the scope of my thoughts here, we had come to see faith primarily as "head" knowledge. We failed to see the need for that faith to penetrate the heart.

The basic tool of religious education at the time was the *Baltimore Catechism.* We had come to think that knowing all the answers in that book made us faithful, faith-filled Catholic Christians. Of course, this is not true. What it did was simply produce people who knew what Catholicism believed. Somehow we forgot that the act of faith is comparable to the human act of falling in love.

It's like going to a computer dating service and getting a printout of the man or woman who possesses all the traits you would want in a partner. No one would suggest that you marry this person right away. All you have is knowledge about the person; now you must come to love the person. It is like this with God. Actually, the *Baltimore Catechism* had solid theological answers. It was our use of the book that created the problem.

Think back to the answer to the question: "Why did God make you?" All of you in my age category know the answer: "God made us to know him, love him and serve him in this world and be happy with him in the next." The sequence is perfect—know God, love God, serve God. But somehow we failed to find a way to the students' hearts.

Roman Catholics today need to learn from their past and appreciate that past. We also need to grow and follow the promptings of the Spirit of God as that Spirit continues to renew and bless us. But we are experiencing a real crisis today among Roman Catholics. I see it every day. I call it a crisis of religious illiteracy. Far too many Catholics really do not know what their church teaches or why.

I know someone who teaches religious education in a local parish. When she brought up the Hail Mary to her fourth-grade students, one boy knew about the Hail Mary but only in reference to the famous Doug Flutie "Hail Mary" football pass. Sadly, he did not know it was also a prayer!

It is hard to appreciate the remarkable moment we now call Vatican II if the post-Vatican II church is the only one you know. I see it every day with my students in the college where I teach. They inherited the renewed church and the self-understanding of what it now means to be a Catholic. As a result, they probably think I have a serious obsession with Vatican II. Or maybe they think I lead such a sheltered life—no friends, no fun, no excitement—that Vatican II has become my hobby!

No matter how they view my love affair with Vatican II, by the end of each semester they are certain of one thing—something extraordinary occurred in the life of the Catholic Church during the four council sessions from 1962–65, something that would affect the church in a way that no other event ever had.

If they happen to be very bright—or just very eager to humor me—my students come to understand that the Second Vatican Council was truly a moment of grace for the church, a clear sign that the Risen Christ was keeping the promise he made at the end of Matthew's gospel: "I am with you always, to the end of the age" (Matthew 28:20). And the promise recorded in John's gospel: "I will ask the Father, and he will give you another Advocate, to be with you forever. This is the Spirit of truth . . . who will teach you everything, and remind you of all that I have said to you" (John 14:16, 26).

It is up to each of us to continue to tell this story. Because, if we do not, then we will fail at our most important task—being signs of hope for the church of the new millennium.

THE BISHOPS OF VATICAN II claimed that the future of humanity lies in the hands of those who are strong enough to give future generations reasons for living and hoping. And given the somewhat somber picture I have painted thus far regarding the failure to successfully implement Vatican II in the last forty years, this task may seem even more daunting.

But, of course, I have a solution! In 1995, my religious congregation, formerly the Dominican Sisters of Newburgh, New York, merged with two other Dominican congregations and formed a new congregation. In what I believe was a moment of grace for us, we agreed to be called the Dominican Sisters of Hope.

It is this virtue of hope that I would like to offer as we try to remember, recapture, and reignite the spirit of Vatican II in our time. It is the reason why the words of Leann Womack's song "I Hope You Dance" seem so appropriate as a backdrop for my thoughts.

Let me share some lines from the song for those who may not be familiar with it:

I hope you never lose your sense of wonder
You get your fill to eat but always keep that hunger
May you never take one single breath for granted
God forbid love ever leave you empty handed
I hope you still feel small when you stand beside
the ocean
Whenever one door closes I hope one more opens
Promise me that you'll give faith a fighting chance
And when you get the choice to sit it out or dance . . .
I hope you dance.

As we reflect on the achievements of Vatican II and express our concerns over why more progress has not been made, I think such words can inspire us. I invite you to continue the dance begun forty years ago, to relive the enthusiastic response to renewal and, most importantly, to find ways to share this response with all those people in our ministries.

A Theology of Hope

Two theological realities form the basis of my invitation to you: the person of Jesus Christ and the rediscovery of the role of the Holy Spirit. Hope cannot be based on emotional mood swings brought about by good or bad developments—no, real hope must be grounded in the good news of Jesus Christ. In the first letter of Peter, we read: "Always be ready to give a defense to anyone who asks for the reasons for the hope that is in you."

These are *my* reasons. I share these insights with you and hope they have meaning for you as well. They are the source of my confidence and enthusiasm for the twenty-first-century church, a church renewed and invigorated by the Second Vatican Council.

First, the person of Jesus Christ—the first source of hope for all of humanity.

Second, the gift of the Holy Spirit—whose role is being rediscovered today.

1. Jesus Christ

I begin with Jesus, the one who first actively showed hope in the darkness of our history. The conditions in which he exercised hope were, in many ways, similar to our own. The kingdom which Jesus announced, and for which he was hoping, would come about only through the abandonment of self to God and absolute trust in the face of opposition and suffering.

Incapable of justifying himself, his reputation apparently lost (at least in the eyes of others), Jesus knew what it would cost not to play the game of the world. But he hoped that extreme love would become the strength for transformation. Because only transformed desire can endure the waiting required of those who hope. Only transformed desire interprets the apparent silence of God as something other than indifference.

Jesus experienced the challenge of being human: he did not mask the failure of his preaching; he wept over Jerusalem; he experienced the pettiness and blindness of the scribes and Pharisees; he witnessed the limitations of his disciples. Yet, Jesus' hope was rooted in the absolute faithfulness of God.

As I noted earlier, the fathers of the Second Vatican Council claimed that the future of humanity lies in the hands of those who are strong enough to provide coming generations with reasons for living and hoping. Christians find these reasons in the Paschal Mystery—the life, death, and resurrection of Jesus Christ. Christians are people set apart by the cross of Christ.

Theologian Gerald O'Collins states: "Only by his great outcry, 'My God, my God, why have you forsaken me?' did Jesus become our brother. This outcry knew the terror of death, but the darkness is faced with the words: "Father, into your hands I commend my spirit."

The ultimate experience and example of human hope begins in the Garden of Gethsemane. Jesus prays: "Father, if this cup could pass . . . not my will, but yours be done." So much of the Old Testament is an account of humanity's failure to truly accept its creaturely status and therefore its failure to truly accept God. Finally, in the person of Jesus, the ultimate human yes is uttered.

If we are to be signs of hope for a new generation in the twenty-first-century church, if we are going to succeed in renewing this church in the spirit of Vatican II, then it will be necessary to ground our commitment in this most complete act of hope. This is what it means to live in the reign of God and hope is the central virtue of anyone living in this reign.

Hope is confidence in the possibility that those things which are destructive of human well-being and spiritual development will be overcome. Without this personal surrender, our hope will remain sterile. We will not succeed in being signs of a renewed church for a new generation. What a lost opportunity that would be!

2. The Rediscovery of the Holy Spirit

We now look to the role of the Holy Spirit in our attempt to continue the dance begun by Vatican II. We need to rediscover the Holy Spirit, just as the fathers of Vatican II managed to do.

Before the Second Vatican Council, we found ourselves at a loss when it came to speaking about the Holy Spirit. We could talk about God the Father—after all, didn't we have pictures of God on little holy cards? And we could speak about the human Jesus, but the Holy Spirit was a real challenge. Of course, we had pictures of the Spirit as well— recall the holy cards showing the little flames over the heads of the apostles on Pentecost.

Happily, thanks to the insights of the council fathers, theologians have come to probe more deeply into the mystery of this member of the Trinity. The Christian God is a God of absolute proximity, a God revealed in the human face of Jesus, a God present in the very depths of our being.

In this regard, there was a wonderful article in *America* magazine a while back entitled: "A God Who Gets Foolishly Close." In it the author writes:

> But now the image that touches me is of a God who
> gets foolishly close. So close, that our joys and

sorrows, our grief and anguish are tightly wrapped with this God. So close we forget this presence. This was the fundamental message of Christ's life. Jesus knew the human condition, but he also knew of the deeper truth waiting to be born. This broken, anxious world is oozing with God . . . this is what Jesus wanted to convey to a searching humanity . . . to encourage us to let God interrupt us, embrace our fragility and our hunger to know our place in this blessed creation.

Such a powerful description of the presence of God in us! Our awareness of this presence is made possible through the gift of the Holy Spirit. Christianity teaches us that we are made by God, for God. This means that humanity was created with a unique capacity for God at the core of its being.

The relationship between nature and grace has been a topic of theological discussion for centuries. During medieval times, there were those who described grace as something "added on" to human nature—sort of like icing on a cake. Theologian Karl Rahner disagreed with this perception. He claimed that as humans, we have a "graced nature" and no separation between the two is possible. (Sometimes when I am explaining this to my students, I use the example of the "whiteness in a piece of chalk." There is no way to separate the two.)

In his first letter to the Corinthians, Saint Paul writes:

There is to be sure a certain wisdom which we express among the spiritually mature . . . . What we utter is God's wisdom. God planned it before all ages for our glory. God has revealed this wisdom through the Spirit . . . God's Spirit, helping us to recognize the gifts we have been given.

Paul seems to be giving an account of what happens when God becomes real for a given human person, when the human spirit becomes conscious of its being touched by the sacred, when it becomes aware of the presence of God within. Like a woman with child, the child is within her before she is even aware of it. So too with God.

In his encyclical, "The Lord and Giver of Life," Pope John Paul II wrote: "Under the influence of the Holy Spirit, the inner spiritual man and woman matures and grows strong. They discover the divine dimension of their being and life."

At the Second Vatican Council, Cardinal Leon-Josef Suenens was asked by a journalist: "What do you think constitutes at the present time the greatest obstacle to the evangelization of the world?"

He responded: "The lack of faith among Christians as to what—by the grace of God—they really are."

Do we ever think about this, about what we really are, about what the presence of God in us enables us to be, to do and to hope for? I think the most serious sin is to refuse to allow the Spirit to act in us, to be a source of deep hope for us. Sinning against the Holy Spirit means no longer believing that God can change our world, because we don't believe that God can change us.

The real atheist is not the one who claims that God does not exist, but the one who denies the Spirit's infinite power to create and transform. If we are to recapture the truly Spirit-filled moment that we call Vatican II, if we are to be signs of promise for those in our care, our hope must be rooted in a belief in the Spirit's ability to continue to change and renew and recreate a new heart in each of us.

Conclusion

Some of us are part of a generation who experienced the church before the Second Vatican Council. In some ways, we have recently witnessed a reversal of fortunes. What have we done wrong?

Is it the fault of Vatican II that attendance at Sunday Mass has declined significantly, that fewer and fewer Catholics receive the sacrament of Penance? Is it the fault of Vatican II that seminaries and convents are half-empty?

Some of us remember the 1950s when our Catholic schools were filled, when there was a nun in every classroom. There are those who *would* blame Vatican II, who would insist that a return to a pre-Vatican II church would solve our current problems.

I do not agree. As suggested by a retreat director in a recent theological article in *The Tablet*, it is time for us to reflect on our current situation in the light of the resurrection and the appearances of the Risen Christ, and to see the disciples as examples for our time.

The New Testament tells us that the Risen Christ was clearly different than the historical Jesus had been. The gospels tell us how the disciples did not recognize him at first. The disciples themselves were profoundly changed by their experience—the shame of abandoning him at Gethsemane, the discovery of their own cowardice and fear, the sobering, maturing experience of despair, and then the realization that, in spite of all this, the Risen Lord was inviting them back to intimacy as well as giving them responsibility for the church that would emerge. Their experience can best be described as a transformation. They and their transformation are role models for us today.

The church of the twenty-first century, whose shape we cannot fully discern at this time, will be new. It can be a resurrected, sobered, mature church. If we who serve the people of God today are experiencing something of a crucifixion, it is in order that we may rise again, entirely by the Spirit of God, to a new place.

Before Vatican II, the church was known for its certitude; things were clearly right or wrong; there were no gray areas; and if we had a question, we had only to look to the pope for an answer. This is one reason why many people were surprised when John XXIII announced the Second Vatican Council. They did not see the need for a dialogue and theological inquiry.

Of course, as recipients of what Vatican II brought about, we now know why John was moved to call the council. Indeed it did spark new life into our church. And we must not let that spark go out.

WE CANNOT FORECAST what the Holy Spirit will do in our time because with the Holy Spirit there are moments when the impossible becomes possible, moments when the unthinkable becomes thinkable.

At the conclave after the death of Pope Pius XII in 1958, the cardinals were having difficulty arriving at a majority candidate for the papacy. Finally, a group decided to put their votes toward Angelo Roncalli. We are told that their thinking at the time was this: "He is quite old. He is a rather simple man. He can serve well as a sort of interim pope. He will make no major changes."

Little did they know what this "peasant" would bring about in the church. It is the reason why we celebrate a *person* who truly was a manifestation of the spirit in our time, why we remember and recapture a *time* when that Spirit was so fruitful in our lives.

But much of the unbounded hope which stirred in the days of Vatican II has faded—we seem to have forgotten how powerful it was. We need to rekindle the hope brought about by Vatican II. We need to demonstrate the remarkable growth that occurred in theology. We need to help the people of God penetrate the deeper meanings still waiting to be explored in the teachings of Vatican II.

As theologian Anthony Padovano has written: "This is the tradition that the transformed apostles leave us . . . a kind of love that always leads us into the future unafraid while bringing us out of the past unharmed." In an article entitled "No Turning Back," Padovano speaks about the apostle Peter after the resurrection. He writes:

> We see Peter for the last time in John's gospel, back in Galilee, with James and John. Easter has already touched their lives. . . they are fishing and there on the shore is the Risen Christ. Peter rushes into the water and is filled with unasked questions. Who are you? You are not the same as I once knew you and yet I know it is you. Peter has questions because Christ is not recognizable, not predictable. It takes more faith to be loyal to such a Christ.
>
> But the consequences of such loyalty is an Easter faith. Peter is silent, looking for signs that his faith is not misplaced or his hope in vain. It will be Peter now who is changed and who becomes the herald of Easter glory.

Padovano goes on to speak of Peter's adjustment and compares it to the adjustment the people of God make in embracing the post-Vatican II church. He says the struggle is worth it and asks: Who would ever go back to our former way of being church?

His reply: only the terrified and the frightened. But we cannot heal them by returning to the rigid certitudes of the past, brought about by fear and insecurity. We lost a version of the church along the way, but we did not lose God.

God makes a covenant with human hearts, not with institutions. The reforms of Vatican II sought to make the Incarnation a human one, an Incarnation of God's presence in human life itself. The Risen Christ is always on the shore of our future hopes where we are invited to come with fewer certitudes but deeper realities.

This is the invitation you and I have been given—to bring the work of the Spirit, Vatican II, to a new generation, to rekindle that fire, to make a new generation aware of the power of God at work in our church. And to paraphrase some words from the song: "I hope you will give Vatican II a fighting chance, if you get the chance to sit it out or dance, I hope you dance."

The church of the new millennium is counting on us.

BIBLIOGRAPHY

McCarthy, Timothy. *The Catholic Tradition: Before and After Vatican II 1878–1994.* Chicago: Loyola University Press, 1994.

Nouwen, Henri. *With Burning Hearts.* Maryknoll: Orbis Books, 1994.

O'Malley, John, S.J. *Tradition and Transition: Historical Perspectives on Vatican* Delaware: Michael Glazier, 1989.

Padovano, Anthony. "No Turning Back," *National Catholic Reporter.* (November 12, 1999): 3–5.

The Greatest Story *Never* Told!

SEVERAL YEARS AGO DURING A PRESENTATION ON Vatican II at Loyola University, Chicago, a young undergrad rushed into the session asking, "Is this the 'Vacation II' workshop?" That student's question gives us a clue to the understanding of an entire generation that has been raised and formed *after* the Second Vatican Council. The reality today, unfortunately, is that very few adults understand Blessed Pope John XXIII's hopes for the council, how it operated, or its outcome. In many ways, Vatican II remains the "greatest story *never* told!"

In the beginning . . .

As we prepared to the celebrate the great Jubilee of the year 2000, Pope John Paul II offered us a vision and planning guidelines in his apostolic letter, *As the Millennium Draws*

Near (Tertio millennio adveniente, November 14, 1994). On the eve of the twenty-first century, the Holy Father reminded us, "The best preparation for the new millennium . . . can only be expressed in a renewed commitment to apply, as faithfully as possible, the teaching of Vatican II to the life of every individual and of the whole Church" (20). Throughout his pontificate, Pope John Paul II has esteemed Vatican II as "the greatest religious event of the twentieth century!"

Yet the Second Vatican Council did not simply fall out of the sky. It enjoys a context that is nothing less than the entire history of the church. From the time of Jesus through each period of the church, history has been shaping the world and making the way for this council of renewal and reform. Like a blooming flower, history allows each period of our past to tell its story and impact the world. If we are honest, we know that some periods have blossomed brighter than others—some bringing fresh energy to the Gospel message, and others thwarting the beauty of God's reign waiting to flourish in the world.

As we explore Vatican II, let us remember (literally recall and make our own again) the wise words of our beloved Pope John XXIII who referred to history as "the great teacher of life." Recalling this Spirit-given wisdom, we must take the time to reread church history, understand its movements, and place Vatican II is its proper context. The council is *not* the final voice of the Spirit to the church in this postmodern world. But seen in the long and varied history of the church, it is a vibrant blossom of faith. Pope John himself said his invoking of the council was "like a flash of heavenly light, shedding sweetness in eyes and hearts." And as Father Virgil Elizondo has prophetically proclaimed, "Vatican II isn't finished, it's just beginning!"

Who Was That Masked Man?

The Holy Spirit is the Spirit of grace and of surprises. No one expected Angelo Roncalli, our beloved, and now blessed, Pope John XXIII, to call a council, including himself. In the eyes of the conclave that elected him supreme pontiff in October of 1958, the elderly Roncalli was to be a pope of "transition." The cardinals who engineered his rise to the Chair of Peter, felt that this aged diplomat would bring a calm to the church after the very busy pontificate of Pius XII. But the Spirit had a gracious surprise in store.

In his diary, *Journal of a Soul,* published after his death, John XXIII wrote: "Everyone was convinced that I would be a provisional and transitional pope." Transitional indeed! With his broad diplomatic and pastoral experience, deep faith, and often remembering his roots as the son of poor share-croppers, John XXIII helped the church in its *transition* (literally "passage" in both Catholic mindset and practice) from a medieval church to one engaged in and committed to the needs of the modern world. Like a farmer in the field, John XXIII planted the seeds of the council and then literally sat back in his papal apartment to watch much of its proceedings develop via closed-circuit television. His was a servant leadership.

Stories and myths of Angelo Roncalli abound. Some are true, yet all carry the truth of the person whose motto was "Listen to everything, forget much, correct a little. Unity in necessary things, freedom in doubtful things, charity in all things."

Blessed Pope John's ability to connect life and faith are well known. During a Mass for fifty couples celebrating their twenty-fifth wedding anniversary, John XXIII reminded them that while the love they shared was like the roses the wives were wearing, it had not been without the *thorns* that accompany roses. All nodded in agreement! In preparing to meet President Eisenhower, John XXIII received English lessons from Monsignor Thomas Ryan, the Irish counselor on staff at the Vatican Secretariat of State. It is said that the few words of greeting he memorized came out with a "bit of the brogue"[1]

When America's First Lady came to Rome, Pope John waited in his library agonizing over one of two alternative greetings recommended by his secretary, "Mrs. Kennedy, Madame," or "Madame, Mrs. Kennedy." But when the library entrance opened and the pope saw her, he raised his arms in welcome and exclaimed: "Jacqueline!"

When asked to share his philosophy of action, John XXIII offered a simple yet powerful French epigram: *"Il faut faire quelque chose; il faut faire faire quelque chose; il faut laisser faire quelque chose,"* that is, there some things one must do oneself, some things one must make others do, and certain things one must leave alone.[2]

Bringing the Council to Life

The four sessions of Vatican II ended on December 8, 1965, leaving the church and the world with sixteen documents of varied length and import. Four constitutions, nine decrees, and three declarations were left in the hands of local bishops to reflect upon and implement. But in most postconciliar dioceses, there was no systematic catechesis on the council's teaching. We had rearranged the furniture, turned altars, and removed communion rails, but we failed to help "Joe and Helen Pew," the average Catholic, to understand what the council was all about.

Don't wait for the movie. Read the book! is my mantra to every Vatican II workshop audience. Rather than review the documents here, however, my goal is to highlight the steps that brought Vatican II to life. If we listen with an "inner ear," to the "inside" story of the council, we will rediscover the principles needed to shape church ministry for decades to come.

One Step at a Time

In his three-volume work, *Vatican II in Plain English*,[3] theologian and author Bill Huebsch describes the steps that brought Pope John XXIII's vision of *aggiornamento* (bringing the Church up to date for today's times, needs, and people) to reality. These steps contain "the greatest story *never* told:"

1. Pope John XXIII Announces the Council

2. Pope John Models *Aggiornamento* with a Synod in Rome

3. Pope John Officially Closes Vatican I

4. Pope John Invites Worldwide Consultation

5. Papal Commissions Draft Schemata for the Council

6. Pope John Issues Council Rules and Procedures

7. The Bishops Arrive in Rome and Open the Council

Pope John XXIII Announces the Council:

"*Si, si! Un Concilio!*" was the response Pope John XXIII received toward the end of 1958 as he discussed the role of the church in the modern world with the late Cardinal Domenico Tardini. When the words "A Council!" suddenly sprang from his lips, Cardinal Tardini's immediate reaction was, "Yes, yes! A Council!"[4]

Trusting the still small voice of the Spirit, Pope John announced his intention to hold only the twenty-first council in church history. This was to be an ecumenical (worldwide) council with 2,908 eligible bishops to be invited. A month later, John XXIII received a completely different response to his inspiration.

While speaking to seventeen cardinals at the basilica of St. Paul Outside the Walls on January 25, 1959, the pope announced three incredible actions. Observing the need to provide an updating of church language and practice to better meet the needs of today, he shared his intention to: (1) hold a synod for the diocese of Rome—remember to be pope is to be bishop of Rome, (2) gather an ecumenical council of the church, and (3) to revise the code of canon law, making it a more useful tool to church pastors.

Pope John described the goal of this council as an *aggiornamento*, (bringing up to date) through (1) an inner renewal of the church, (2) a fresh representation of the church's essence—the very nature of what it means to *be* church, and (3) a commitment to unity in the body of Christ.

Turning to the cardinals gathered, John XXIII said, "I would like to have your advice." To a man, each cardinal sat silent, not uttering a single word of response. In his diary, the pope recorded his disappointment: "Humanly we could have expected that the cardinals, after hearing our allocution, might have crowded around to express approval and good wishes. . . . Instead there was a devout and impressive silence," he wrote. "Explanation came on following days. . . ."[5]

You see, the members of the Roman Curia, those offices responsible for the day-to-day running of the church, didn't believe a council was necessary. And, they didn't believe that the pope quite understood the world like they did.

Many Curia members feared that the growing liturgical movement in Europe, Canada, and the Midwestern United States, which was influenced by Lambert Beaudin, O.S.B., (Belgium 1903); Virgil Michael, O.S.B., (St. John's in Collegeville, Minnesota, 1925); and Romano Guardini at the Benedictine Abbey of Beron in Tübingen—as early as 1915 Guardini had turned the altar away from the wall and seated the assembly on three sides. The curia also considered the new approach to biblical study dangerous. Even if this historical-critical method was based on Pope Pius XII's own *Divino Afflante Spiritu.*

Pope John did not share this vision of fear and often reminded his staff that history is "the great teacher of life." With his wisdom we could look honestly into the past and face the future with faith not fear.

Principle for Today: Listen hard and discern with others. Trust the voice of the Spirit and act upon it!

Pope John Models *Aggiornamento* with a Synod in Rome

As the bishop of Rome, Pope John gathered his flock for a week of reflection and renewal. During the week of January 24 to January 31, 1960, in his proper cathedral, the basilica of St. John Lateran, the pope modeled to his brother bishops how this *aggiornamento* would work—from the inside out!

Doing most of the talking himself, John XXIII did not preach on whether the sign of the cross can be made with the left or right hand, or if a reverent bow from the waist "counts" as much as a genuflection. There are those who still argue about these things today!

Setting an example for the rest of the church, Pope John preached on the *central* mysteries of the Christian faith: belief in God as a Trinity of love; redemption from sin by the human trials and death of Jesus; the resurrection and our longing (hope) to see God "face to face." He was also candid about the pitfalls and potential dangers of life in the modern world.

Pope John chose compassion above the law in regard to priests who left the Church, offering them "the mercy of the Lord and the humaneness and decency of ecclesiastical superiors."[6] This was a revolutionary shift and one drafted by John XXIII himself.

When the synodal documents were submitted they followed the style of typical canonical legislation, to which several Vatican canonists retorted, "That's not law!" The pope's reply was simple, "It's not intended as a strictly legal document." In John XXIII's mind and heart this synod's proclamation was meant to be a *vade mecum*, a guide for Christian living.[7] Completing the Synod of Rome, the pope turned his attention to the ecumenical council.

> **Principle for Today:** If genuine renewal comes from the "inside out," then stay close to home and take care of business. Stick to the important things, not only the urgent ones!

Pope John Officially Closes Vatican I

As a historian, John XXIII knew it was important to mark the moment. On December 7, 1959 during an allocution in the Basilica of the Twelve Apostles, the pope announced that his council would be called "Vatican II." This public and solemn proclamation ended the hopes of some church leaders that Vatican II would be a continuation of Vatican I, which lacked an official ending due to the Franco-Prussian war (1869–70). Now the official preparations for Vatican II could begin.[8]

Principle for Today: Notice when one door closes and another opens. Take the time to mark these moments.

Pope John Invites Worldwide Consultation

With vigorous opposition from his own curial staff, Pope John's office issued invitations to the world's 2,500 residential bishops asking them to provide pastoral issues and council agenda items. More than 2,000 bishops responded. Because there was no limitation on the matters which could be presented or the manner in dealing with these issues, the pope gained access to the real minds and hearts of the world's bishops.[9]

Principle for Today: Be careful what you ask for. You may get it! Open consultation will put you in touch with real needs and the solutions to meet them.

Papal Commissions Draft Schemata for the Council

During this preparatory period, from June of 1960 to September of 1962, Pope John established commissions with cardinals, bishops, and other church staff to prepare working drafts. Curia members, who were very much against the idea of a council, were told by the pope to concern themselves with the day-to-day running of the church. The operation of the council was be in the hands of a central commission not attached to the Curia. This became an open sore for the Curia who worked behind the scenes to at least control the discussion with a group of conservative cardinals.[10]

The stage was set for the great debates that gave life and breath to Vatican II.

> **Principle for Today:** You can't control the Holy Spirit, so learn to cooperate.

Pope John Issues Council Rules and Procedures

Five weeks before the council opened, on September 5, 1962, the pope sent rules to the council attendees which:

1. Named a presiding council that shared and rotated leadership during the working sessions, and appointed heads of the commissions in charge of the working documents.

   > **Principle for Today:** Shared and rotated leadership gets things done.

2. Required a two-thirds majority vote prior to his own approval.

   > **Principle for Today:** Listen to the majority, but invite everyone to come along.

3. Invited observers who were non-Catholic to attend, (a first for the church).

   > **Principle for Today:** It's never too late to say "I'm sorry!"

4. Required the bishops to stay in Rome for the completion of each session—this did not allow a bishop to "vote with his feet" and go home.

Principle for Today: Be true to the process. Reaching consensus is work, but stay the course and you'll get there.

5. Gave specific directions on attire, required a profession of faith, and an oath of secrecy.

   Principle for Today: Belonging is important. Make sure the rules are clear.

6. Directed that Latin was to be used in public sessions while allowing local languages in the commissions.

   Principle for Today: Remove any obstacles for full, conscious, and active participation.

7. Provided an open discussion format: a topic would be introduced; speeches could be made in favor or opposition; speeches had to stick to the topic at hand, be in Latin, and could not be more than ten minutes in length. (Note: The three-volume *Council Daybooks* provide an accurate account of the speeches and debates of each session.)

   Principle for Today: The process is everything. The more open you are, the more open you'll become!

The Bishops Arrive and Open the Council

From eyewitness accounts, the morning of October 11, 1962 was a "glorious Roman day." In a scene that Cecil B. De Mille would have been hard pressed to create, nearly 2,500 bishops (500 from South America, 126 native Asians, 118 native

Africans) processed across the papal square into the great aula of St. Peter's Basilica.

On that historic day, the prelates celebrated the Mass of the Holy Spirit in Latin and in Greek to affirm Eastern and Western unity. Then, in a homily that rocked the world, the pope began by saying he was tired of his advisors' negative tones: "Though burning with zeal," he said, these men "are not endowed with very much sense of discretion or measure." And reminding all present that history is the great teacher of life, the pope continued: "We feel we must disagree with these prophets of doom, who are always forecasting disaster, as though the end of the world were at hand." [11]

The real goal of the council was about to become clear: "Divine Providence," said the pope, "is leading us to a new order in human relations." Echoing an imperative of the Holy Spirit, John XXIII said that the church must "...bring herself up to date where required," and that "she must ever look to the present, to new conditions and new forms of life introduced into the modern world, which have opened new avenues to the Catholic apostolate." [12]

Challenging the church to take a step forward in mining the richness of its teachings, the pope boldly stated: "The substance of the ancient doctrine of faith (*depositum fidei*) is one thing; the way in which it is expressed is another." According to Pope John, the real task of this council was to find the best solutions (formulas) for *our* time. We were to reverence (to take notice of) the past, but not be slaves to it!

The pope concluded his vision of renewal and reform by calling for the use of the "medicine of mercy rather than of severity," and that our approach to restoring visible unity in the entire Christian family was to embrace not only Christians but "those who follow non-Christian religions," with "the fullness of charity." [13] Love was to be our vocation.

Principle for Today: Now that you've heard a bit of the "inside story," become familiar with the sixteen documents of Vatican II. Don't wait for the movie. . . . Read the Book!

On to the Other Shore

On my first very day of graduate school, I slumbered into a course on Christian anthropology. Seated in a small class and basking in a rare Seattle sun, I listened to our professors, Father John Heagle and Sister Fran Ferder, F.S.P.A., give instructions: "Good morning. Our class will begin today down on the waterfront. You may leave your books and backpacks here, but we will meet at the Pier." We all looked at each other and wondered what was up. Off we trudged, down the steep Seattle hills to the emerald green of Puget Sound.

Meeting Father John and Sister Fran at the Pier, each student was handed a ferry ticket and asked to board—no instructions! Once the ferry had set sail for Bainbridge Island, Father John gathered the class for some introductory remarks. I will never forget these words of wisdom: "This is the Church, this ferry and all of us on it. Since the Second Vatican Council we have left the shore and the safety of what has been. We are moving on to the "other shore" which is the already-and-not-yet Reign of God. Our task as baptized people of God is to be faithful to Christ, to the church, and to the journey of faith." We resumed regular classes the following day filled with a vision for the future.

Nine days after the opening of the Second Vatican Council, Pope John asked the council fathers to issue a "message to humanity." The pope wanted the world to know what was happening at the council and what it was all about.

May these Spirit-guided words from Vatican II echo on our lips as we help the church move on to "the other shore": "In this assembly, under the guidance of the Holy Spirit, we wish to inquire how we ought to renew ourselves. So that we may be found increasingly faithful to the Gospel of Jesus Christ." [14]

Sources

A Concise History of the Catholic Church, Thomas Bokenkotter, Image Books: New York, 1979.

Council Daybook, Vatican II, Sessions 1–4, Floyd Anderson, editor, National Catholic Welfare Conference: Washington, DC, 1966.

The Documents of Vatican II, Walter M. Abbott, S.J., general editor, The American Press: New York, 1966.

History of Vatican II: Volume I, Joseph A. Komanchak, English version editor, Orbis Press: Maryknoll, NY, 1995.

The New Cambridge Modern History: The Reformation: 1520–1559, G.R. Elton, editor, Cambridge University Press: London, 1979.

Vatican Council II, Xavier Rynne, Farrar, Straus, and Giroux, Inc.: New York, 1968.

Vatican II in Plain English, The Council, Bill Huebsch, Thomas More Publishing: Allen, Texas, 1996.

1. Xavier Rynne, *Vatican Council II,* Farrar, Straus, and Giroux: New York, 1968, p.5.
2. Rynne, p.5.
3. Thomas More: Allen, Texas, 1996.
4. Rynne, p. 3.
5. Rynne. p.4.
6. Synod article 35, Rynne pp. 26–27.
7. Rynne, p.26.
8. Joseph A. Komanchak, ed., *History of Vatican II,* volume 1, American Press: New York, 1995, p. 51.
9. Rynne, p. 28.
10. Rynne, p. 32.
11. Rynne, p. 46.
12. Rynne, p. 47.
13. Rynne, p. 48.
14. Message to Humanity, #3.

Reading the Signs of the Times in Faith

READING THE SIGNS OF THE TIMES IS THE TASK and the gift of the prophet, and we are indeed called to be a prophetic people. What does it take to be a prophet? Prophecy has two aspects, one turned to God in receptivity to divine revelation, and the other turned to the world about us. It was the genius of Vatican II, and especially of *Gaudium et spes (The Pastoral Constitution on the Church in the Modern World)* to recognize this and realize that people need a lot of guidance in learning how to do this in the highly complex modern world in which we live.

To bring into a calm and clear-headed relationship what we know from constant receptivity to God with what we can learn progressively about the affairs of our world involves a finely honed art of discernment. And beyond discernment it requires prudent and disciplined decisions about when, where, and how to speak up and to act. How are we to learn this? We know as Christians that our central model for this is the person of Jesus, and that our main source for knowing how Jesus focused his life, judgments and relationships is in the gospels of the New Testament.

But we do not walk through the complex modern world equipped only with a Bible and our individual intelligence and good will. We are heirs of a rich tradition of discipleship in all kinds of cultures and situations. Moreover, we have the support of a community of disciples held together in a common liturgy and a common goal. And we who live at this particular time in history have had much of this laid out in its many implications for our world today by the Second Vatican Council.

Many in the Catholic community of our times are discouraged by certain scandals, and by an apparent reversal from the Roman Curia of much that was gained in clarity, immediacy, and gospel simplicity. Yet we should not fail to acknowledge and appreciate the great gifts that came to us from the Second Vatican Council, bearing fruit in the community even in the face of panic-driven efforts to domesticate the Holy Spirit of God and reverse the trends. What, after all, did Vatican II offer the laity, the baptized, the people who are church?

In the first place, there was the return to Scripture, both in the *Dogmatic Constitution on Divine Revelation*, and especially in the *Constitution on the Sacred Liturgy*. For all of us who take part in the Sunday liturgy regularly, a far greater and better-arranged selection of texts is kept steadily before us. Even while we were unaware of it, this has been building in the Catholic community a common store of narratives and symbols, a common memory around which our experienced tradition is being reshaped.

Many ordinary Catholics have found encouragement and opportunity to read Scripture daily on their own, to go to classes and lectures to help them read with understanding, and to band together in various types of small communities that read and discuss Scripture together. This has been an immense enrichment, which no strictures from the Vatican can spoil or diminish. Those too young to remember the pre-Vatican II church must take our word for it: the life and spirituality in the Catholic community of the 1930s, 1940s and 1950s had a very different flavor. It was based not directly on Scripture but on the catechism, useful enough in itself but bare survival rations for Christian spirituality.

Beyond this, Vatican II gave us a renewal, a reinvigoration and new translucency of the liturgy. There are now so many and such rich reasons to participate that go far beyond avoiding mortal sin, obeying a church law, and individually receiving the gift of Christ's presence in Holy Communion. The whole liturgy of the church, but especially the Sunday Eucharist, has opened up lively active participation of the whole people. Whether they advert to it or not, it has become their worship, their transformation, their building of the community of the Resurrection in the world. And what is experienced in the liturgy models the vocation of the laity in the world. We are not called into the community of the Resurrection, the community of the disciples of Jesus, to be kept safe from the world as some privileged group, but precisely to go out and transform the world wherever it does not reflect the glory of its creator.

This is perhaps the greatest "conversion" of the Catholic Church in the Second Vatican Council: it became critical of its self-preoccupation and turned outward. In the *Decree on the Apostolate of the Laity*, in the *Dogmatic Constitution on the Church*, and perhaps most of all in the *Pastoral Constitution on the Church in the Modern World*, there is a concern with mission, with having a task in the world. This task is in the main the challenge to the laity. It is a challenge to prophetic discernment and creative action. It is a challenge to an apostolic and alert Christian life that cannot be blueprinted— a life not lived by waiting for hierarchic instructions, and certainly not by staying out of risky or confused situations.

What the joint discernment of the bishops of all the local churches, generally guided by their advisers of varied expertise from the local churches, offers in these documents is not blue- printed or programmatic but discerning of the great categories of need in our times and challenging toward many initiatives, many creative responses. We realized in the wake of Vatican II that a truly prophetic church must be a church in which initiatives come from the local communities. It is they who can discern in their experience what is happening in the world, and it is they who can bring the light of the Gospel to bear on the needs and problems in their own sphere of life and activity.

If the initiative must come from the local communities, then it must come from us, from all of us in our various contexts. And if it is to come from all of us, then we must be aware of our calling, constantly tuned in to divine revelation but also constantly tuned in to the world about us. Our discernments must be guided by the wisdom of the community and its multi-stranded tradition—much larger than Canon Law, much fuller than official doctrinal and moral teaching.

All this has come to us in these forty years of grace. We have seen an extraordinary awakening of the church as the People of God. Even if it has happened more clearly in some places than in others, the precedents and the models are there to keep the "dangerous memories" alive in the world where those with hunger in their hearts will meet them. We have seen the Scriptures broken wide open for God's people to draw their vision and inspiration from them. Even if there are attempts to deprive the people of the translations that truly speak to them in their own idiom, even if not all have been encouraged to delve into Scripture for their spiritual sustenance, the flame has been lit and the wind of the Spirit blows where it will, evading all efforts to catch it and box it in.

The blossoming of Scripture and liturgy among the laity has had great fruits. It is not only that growing numbers of lay Catholics have woken to their active role in the work of the redemption. It is not only that a passion for social justice in the world has caught on, especially but not only among the young and the educated in many places. Underlying this is a new realization among many of the Catholic faithful: their Catholic faith is not primarily a matter of intellectual assent to a series of propositions, no matter how fruitful or sublime. It is continual and progressive openness to the continual and progressive divine self-revelation as it comes in many ways in our experience in the world. This is a profound development of Christian maturity. It is something to be welcomed with gratitude, not greeted with anxiety and attempts to set the clock back to a time when things looked tidier.

Then what are we to make of the fact that we have experienced in recent years just such a reaction of concern to tidy things back to where they were, to centralize controls over language, over theologians, over the teaching of local bishops, over independent Catholic institutions, associations and initiatives of all kinds? What are we to make of the great anxiety to guard the designation "Catholic" as the patented institutional trademark, to be used only with official permission?

We are certainly in a time of tension. It is a time of great possibilities and also of great risks. Some among us are discouraged; some have left in a public exodus; others have quietly defected in place without fanfare. But it is noteworthy that the great Catholic community, the Sunday morning crowd and even the Christmas and Easter only crowd, remains rooted because it is their church, their home, their tradition. The curial officials, who send out their restrictive edicts as though they in fact controlled the world, come and go, live and work for a while and grow old, have heart attacks, and pass on. The great community of the faithful prays and stays and makes itself at home for generation after generation, and century after century. There is always fertile ground for new growth, new awakening of life. There is always room for new beginnings in the waking of the Holy Spirit in the community and the stirrings of the prophetic calling.

SO WHAT SHOULD WE BE DOING to foster this? It seems to me that there are chiefly seven strands of a good response to the challenge. In the first place, we need to pray without ceasing in that way of praying that is not primarily talking but primarily listening. We need to do it with Scripture and with the Liturgy; we need to do it in the depths of our own awareness and in true dialogue with the needs of others; but we also need to do it with the newspaper and the television screen.

In the second place we, who are educated and have such ready access to knowledge, need to join with others bringing their specific expertise to study what is really going on in our world. We know too little of the chains of cause and effect that make people poor, angry, despairing, violent, and reckless, both individually and in great masses of population. We know even less of the policies and points of intervention that could genuinely make a difference. Research is generally funded by those who profit from the imbalances and oppressions of human society. Scholarship is usually directed to making the existing systems function more smoothly. The documents of Vatican II, and especially the *Pastoral Constitution on the Church in the Modern World*, continually challenge us to bring the vision of Jesus into the complexities of the modern world, bringing to the task the competences of the modern world.

In the third place, I think we need to make more efforts to appropriate for ourselves and pass on to others the Christian, and particularly the Catholic, intellectual and cultural heritage so that we are not always starting again at the raw beginnings of every effort. All of us are called in some sense to be pioneers in a world that changes so rapidly and presents new questions and challenges. But successful pioneers bring a personally assimilated cultural heritage with them, in which they are sufficiently at home and secure that they know where and how to adapt and innovate.

In the fourth place, this means that we need to be more concerned with history than is generally the case in this society. It is out of intensive historical research in many monasteries that the wonderful renewal of the liturgy came. Those who welcomed this renewal were generally those who had some knowledge and understanding of its roots in the long history of the Christian people and their worship. Those who resisted the renewal of the liturgy were generally people without such a grasp of the historical roots. Deprived in this way, they had no criteria to discern what was true to the tradition and what was a betrayal of the tradition. Without criteria they found it safer to resist change. The resounding endorsement of the apostolic vocation of the baptized came out of many decades of historical work by Yves Congar and other Dominican scholars. Knowing what they had charted concerning the life of the laity and the lay movements through the centuries laid the groundwork for a credible theology of the laity at Vatican II. Those with no historical perspective on this were of course inclined to see only danger in lay initiatives not tightly controlled by hierarchic authority.

In the fifth place, I propose the importance for all of us of reflecting on our implicit ecclesiologies and making them explicit for careful examination. It seems to me that in many of the apparently intractable conflicts within the church at large, and within parishes and groups involved in Catholic activities of all sorts, there is a "hidden agenda," an unrecognized underlying disagreement over our understanding of what is the essence of the church. We can spell it out in a way that everyone will quickly agree with. We can offer the many biblical images, and sum it up that the church is the visible union of the followers of Jesus with him and with one another in a continuity that goes back to the apostolic age. But when we have said that we have thrown a blanket over a great many potential disagreements.

As theologian and Cardinal Avery Dulles has shown, there are many "models" operative in the way Christians think about the church, and those who use them are not necessarily aware of each one's underlying model. A particularly strong tension in the Catholic community in our time seems to be the following. Some see the structural, institutional, externally visible and enforceable manifestations of the church as its "divine element" and what people do with these structures as the "human element." Many after Vatican II, however, have come to see these structures precisely as the human element, whose development can be traced historically to responses at particular times to particular circumstances. What they then see as the divine element is threefold: the call of the eternal Creator God, the initiating and impelling presence of the incarnate Divine Word, and the quickening, empowering, breath of the holy and prophetic Spirit of God, moving to the transformation of the world.

In the sixth place, I propose that we need to do this also in relation to recognizing and acknowledging our implicit soteriologies. In other words, what do we think redemption is? Practically speaking, of what does it consist? It seems to me that the great underlying tension in this respect is as follows.

Since the Constantinian establishment in the Byzantine Empire, followed by the relationship of Charlemagne's empire with the See of Rome, carried to the Catholic colonies on other continents at the beginning of the modern era, there has been a reductionist tendency. It was a tendency to think about salvation only with reference to afterlife, outside of the world, and in purely individual terms. For those who think in that way, concern about social justice, about transformation of the structures that control people's lives in the world, may seem a distraction from the real concern for salvation "of souls."

The return to Scripture, however, as the primary source for our faith, hope, and charity, combined with better knowledge of the early centuries of Christian history, and the outspoken social concerns of the Second Vatican Council, has refocused the attention of many Catholics in their understanding of salvation. While certainly admitting that salvation concerns individuals and that Christian hope reaches beyond death, these Catholics have become more aware that it is all creation that needs to be rescued (redeemed) and made whole (saved). This suggests a focus on transformation of the world with all the relationships, societal structures and uses of the created universe. This is of course inseparably connected with the conversion of individuals, but in reciprocity that requires concern both with societal structures and with individuals.

We need, I think to discover and acknowledge not only where we differ in our understanding but also that people who hold the position that differs from our own can be totally sincere and dedicated to doing the will of God in their lives.

My seventh and last point is the significance of being totally honest with ourselves. We have seen too much of pious pretense, of more concern with preserving a good image of the church than with dealing with the reality. We have seen a certain servile quality in the relation of laity to the clergy, of the clergy in relation to their bishops, and of the bishops in our contemporary society toward the Roman Curia. This is not the freedom of the children of God to which we are called. Yet we have all been influenced to some extent in our upbringing and our experience of life in the Catholic Church with the need to be the approved kind of pious person, rather than the need to acknowledge our own reality in the presence of God.

We have all learned, like Adam and Eve in the story of the garden, to put on the right kind of clothes to conceal who we really are. It is part of the condition of the inescapable influence of original sin in a partly but pervasively distorted history. But it does not need to be deliberately institutionalized in the structures of the church. Nor, when it is so institutionalized, does it provide a good model for being a Catholic Christian. God is truth, and God is greater than any human authority whatsoever.

We are living in a graced time, a time of great challenge. We should be immensely grateful, and live our prophetic vocation with confidence, courage and enthusiasm in the name of Christ, our Lord.

The Roadmap
for the Journey

MY YOUNGER SISTER MAUREEN OFTEN SAID TO ME when we were both in high school: "How can you stand history? It is so boring. It's just names and dates. I hate it!" I would reply: "It isn't boring. It's exciting. It's stories about people and events. You just haven't had the right teachers yet!"

I had been fortunate in grade school and in my early days in high school to have teachers who saw history in that manner. Because of that, when I was assigned as the chaplain at Our Lady of Good Counsel High School and asked to teach church history, I knew that I wanted to teach history through stories. I have had the opportunity to give mini-sessions of church history for RCIA classes and I have found that the students were always excited and desiring of learning more history if I could "whet their appetite" with stories.

Believing that as Catholics we are woefully unaware of our history as a church, I want to share some stories of one of the most significant events in the history of our church so that you might want to learn more. This event is the Second Vatican Council.

The stories are about an event and a person. The person and the event cannot be separated because they are intimately connected in one story.

On October 11, 1962 (memorizing this date is not important!), an event began that was one of the most important experiences in the history of the church since Pentecost. The greatest number of bishops to ever assemble in a church council processed through St. Peter's Square into the largest church in the world. Carried at the end of the procession in a throne held up above the heads of the throngs of people gathered there, was Pope (now Blessed) John XXIII.

When Pope John entered St. Peter's, he disembarked from the throne and walked the length of the church to the main altar. Here he intoned the *Veni Creator* (a hymn in which we call upon the presence of the Holy Spirit to lead us). There was then a Mass celebrated by one of the cardinals during which the gospel was proclaimed in Greek and in Latin. At the conclusion of the Mass, the book containing the gospels was solemnly enthroned in a place of prominence. This enthronement would begin every session of the council to show that Christ was present and presiding over the work being done there.

At the end of this three-hour ceremony, Pope John gave a talk that was to set the tone for the council. Every Catholic should read this discourse. It's entitled *Gaudet Mater Ecclesia* (Mother Church Rejoice). In typical fashion, the pope described his comments as a little "flour from my sack." It was a talk that flowed from a lifetime of experience as priest and pastor.

He reminded the assembly that councils are "celebrations of the union between Christ and his Church." He offered the hope that "with suitable updating and the wise organization of mutual collaboration, the Church will help persons, families, and peoples truly to orient their spirits toward heavenly matters." With characteristic optimism, he nevertheless addressed the opposition that existed to the idea of a council. He stated that there were those who "see the modern world as nothing but deceit and ruin." To them he said: "We feel that we must disagree with these prophets of misfortune." He continued: "Everything, even disagreement, leads to a greater good for the Church."

He assured the council members that this council had not been called "to discuss one or another article of basic Church doctrine that has repeatedly been taught by ancient and modern fathers and theologians." He stated: "A Council is not needed for this." He proclaimed that in this moment, the church prefers "the medicine of mercy rather than that of severity." In choosing the method, the council will be "showing the validity of her doctrines, rather than issuing condemnations."

In a call to all peoples, Pope John said: "The Church . . . wants to show herself as a loving mother to all—kind, patient, full of mercy and goodness, even toward the children who are separated from her." He reminded the assembly that the church was in their hands, coming as they did from all parts of the world. He encouraged them to know that the saints of heaven were with them as protection and that the people of the earth looked to them for inspiration and guidance. He closed by reminding them that success in the work placed before them would require "serenity of mind, brotherly concord, moderation in proposals, and wisdom in deliberation."

It is interesting to note that this speech was reported in the *L'Osservatore Romano*, the official newspaper of the Vatican, but it was changed. Subtle changes in the text gave it a less forward-looking thrust and in some cases actually changed the meaning that the Holy Father had intended.

Pope John did not correct or complain to the editor, he simply used his original text whenever he quoted his talk.

In the evening of that day, there was a gathering in St. Peter's Square. It was not expected that Pope John would be present but he appeared on the balcony of his window and gave an impromptu talk. It is one of his most famous and most quoted talks. He told the crowd that a great day was concluding. He shared with them a concept that had guided him since his youth: attribute all merit to God and give little consideration to self.

> It is your brother who speaks to you, a brother who has become your father by the will of our Lord. But all of this—fatherhood, brotherhood—is a grace of God. Everything, everything! Let us continue to love one another, to love one another like this. Let us go ahead, making use of what unites us, leaving aside whatever could place us in some difficulty, if there is any. We are brothers.

He closed with these words that, even now, find a home in the hearts of those seeking comfort for life's journey:

> When you return home to your children, give them a caress and say, "this caress is from the pope." Perhaps you will find some tears to dry. Comfort those who are suffering. Let them know that the pope is with his children, especially in their times of sadness and bitterness.

TO UNDERSTAND THE STORY of the council, this story had to be told first because it helps us to appreciate the change in the way people perceived the pope and the church before and after the council. Following the council, Catholics came to view the church as more than the hierarchy and saw the hierarchy as representatives of a loving and caring God.

Pope John made it clear in his opening address that he wanted the council to have a free and open discussion and so he would not attend the sessions. He did, however, follow the event by close-circuit TV in his apartment. From there he watched the first working session of the council as a small but vocal group of bishops challenged the agenda that the preparatory committees and the Curia (the various offices in the Vatican) had developed for the council. It was thought by some that the bishops would simply vote on these proposals and then go home. However, in the first fifteen minutes, it was proposed and passed by vote that the bishops should meet in language groups and get to know each other. Then they would choose members for different commissions. Some of the schemas (topics for discussion and vote) were sent back for reworking. Some were rejected outright.

Pope John, while refraining from attending, did enjoy this interaction of the bishops. He saw this as the "working of the Holy Spirit" in leading the council. Only twice, on matters of procedures, did he intervene to change a rule that had been set up before the sessions. If following it seemed in the working of the council to impede rather than help in open discussion, Pope John preferred to allow the member the freedom to speak openly.

There was much discussion about Latin being the language of the council. The pope was not a Latin scholar but, like most priests of his age, he was familiar with Latin as the language of the liturgy and also as the official language of the church. He could use it for communication but he recognized that it was a problem for some of the bishops. Cardinal Richard Cushing of Boston was fluent in Latin but proposed that a multilanguage translation system similar to that used at the United Nations be installed. He was even willing to find a donor who would cover the cost. The idea was rejected.

While rejecting some advancement, the council did have a modern manner of tabulating the votes. They used computer cards. (Remember that this was the early days of computer use!) To vote for a proposal, the member would mark with a pen next to the Latin word *Placet* (which means "it pleases") or to vote against, one would mark next to the words *Non Placet* ("it does not please"). There were about 2,200 voting members of the council at a session. During the four sessions, one and a half million votes were tabulated. During the first session, one of the bishops consistently put two marks on each of the ballots. He voted *Placet* and *Non Placet* on every issue. Although ushers came to know who he was and explained his error to him, he continued to vote this way throughout the first session.

ANOTHER EVENT that occurred toward the end of the first session of the council illustrates the compassionate spirit of good Pope John.

Bishop Peter Cule, from Yugoslavia addressed the council. He gave a long talk in which he suggested that devotion to Saint Joseph should be stressed. Since God had entrusted the care of Jesus to Saint Joseph, the council should entrust the church to his care. Like all the talks, it was in Latin. However, Bishop Cule spoke haltingly and in a nervous manner, sometimes seeming to lose his place. On the podium there were three lights, green, yellow, and red. When the yellow came on, the speaker was to begin his conclusion and he was to stop once the red came on. The bishop continued past his allotted time. Because he was hard to understand, the bishops lost patience with his ramblings and began to call for him to stop. The president of the council finally interrupted him and said, "Complete your holy and eloquent speech. We all love Saint Joseph." The bishop did not stop and so the president turned off the microphone and the bishop returned to his seat with his speech unfinished.

Pope John was watching on the TV and saw what happened. He knew the bishop personally from the Pope's time as a Vatican diplomat in Eastern Europe. He knew that the bishop's speech problem resulted from four years spent in a concentration camp and from his torture at the hands of Communists. He knew that the authorities had made it very difficult for the bishop to even come to the council.

The pope never addressed the bad treatment of the bishop by his fellow bishops. However, three days after the speech, Pope John announced that, effective December 8, 1962, the name of Saint Joseph was to be inserted in the canon of the Mass and that a new petition, "for St. Joseph, her most chaste spouse" would be added to the Divine Praises.

With the death of Pope John on June 3, 1963, the council stopped. On June 21, Cardinal Giovanni Montini was elected pope and chose the name Paul VI. On June 22, he announced that the council would continue and the next session would convene on September 29, 1963. On October 22, in an address to the council, Cardinal Leon-Josef Suenens of Belgium suggested that there should be more laypersons at the council and that among them should be women: "Unless I am mistaken, women make up one half of the world's population." While his comment got much publicity, it was not until the third session that women (for the first time in the history of the church) attended a church council.

A year ago, I was fortunate to have the opportunity to interview one of the fifteen women auditors (that means they could listen but they couldn't speak) at the Second Vatican Council. Her name is Sister Mary Luke Tobin. She is a Sister of Loretto in Kentucky and was, at that time, president of the Conference of Major Religious Superiors of Women's Institutes of America. She was kind enough to share many wonderful stories of her experience.

She told me of her first day at the council. The women had wonderful seats—right near those of the non-Catholic observers. They could hear and see everything. At midmorning, there was a short break when people could stand and stretch. She saw an old friend, Father Gerard Sloyan, who was at the council as a *peritus* (a theologian who assisted a bishop). He asked her to join him for a cup of coffee. There had been built below the "bleachers" that served as the seats where the council fathers sat, a coffee bar that was dubbed "Bar Jonah." It was called this as a play upon the description of St. Peter as the son of John. It says in the gospel of Matthew (16:17), "Blessed are you, Simon bar Jonah."

At this coffee bar Sister Tobin met a number of bishops and chatted before the session started again.

The next day, as the break was beginning, sister headed toward the coffee bar. There a gloved usher in a tuxedo met her. He directed her to a newly created section of the coffee bar in which the women auditors were to have their coffee secluded from the clergy. Sister said they named their section "Bar Nun."

NOW, HONESTLY, aren't you sad to see that this article is coming to an end? I'm hoping that after reading my article (and the other articles in this book) you want to know even more about the history and people of Vatican II. You can do this by reading some of the wonderful histories, personal reflections, and excellent biographies of some of the personalities who attended the council. Videos, books, and even websites can make this exciting period in the history of the church real to us. (For starters, check out the reading list at the end of this volume.)

I invite you to continue this journey begun by Jesus and his followers that is called church history. Take nothing for the road but the stories; and add your own.

Deciding on Reform in the Roman Catholic Church

The Method Used at Vatican II and How It Might Be Used Today

IN HIS OPENING SPEECH AT THE SECOND Vatican Council on October 11, 1962, Pope John said that the council would employ *opportuni aggiornamenti,* Italian words which mean "an appropriate bringing-up-to-date." Used as it was in his speech, the phrase implied that "correction" was being called for in the church's life. (The pope spoke, of course, in Latin in his opening speech. These words in Latin are *opportunis emendationibus,* (paragraph 37) and may be rendered in English as "appropriate corrections.") The phrase suggests a reform of the church itself, rather than merely of the spirituality of its members. In other words, Pope John was suggesting that it was time to introduce "appropriate corrective measures" into the current life of the church. Mild as this seems, it was a major move forward in church thinking. There had simply been no consideration of "correction" in the recent past. No such bringing up to date of anything in the church had been officially sanctioned like this since the Council of Trent in the sixteenth century ended all previous efforts toward that end.

While the notion of *aggiornamento* struck the conservatives and the members of the Roman Curia with fear and outright alarm, it was seized upon by the progressives as a signal to proceed with a reform agenda at this council.

And reform is what we got. Corrections were felt almost immediately right in the pews of the church, among the faithful who'd knelt there for centuries. The corrections ran wide: the rites for every sacrament were reinvented, most of the church's disciplines such as abstinence and fasting underwent modification, and the massive quilt of Catholic devotional life was greatly reduced in size. But the corrections also ran deep and included the role of bishops in governing the church, the theology of grace, the concept of religious liberty, and relationships to Protestants and Jews.

Not surprisingly, this threw the church into some degree of turbulence. There had been so little correction for so long—and now so much came so quickly and with so little explanation to the faithful. The turbulence resulted in part from the speed with which cosmetic liturgical reforms were enacted, but it also had a deeper root.

The corrections and reforms of Vatican II created chaos for average Catholics, including average Catholic clergy, because the church had absolutely no experience changing itself. Prior to this council, the church was seen as identical to the "kingdom of God." As such, it was seen to be free of error and in need of no correction whatsoever.

We had, therefore, established no method or clear process which could be understood and followed to enact the *aggiornamento* for which the pope was now calling. We simply had no pattern of previous corrections within anyone's memory.

This being true, we were confronted with a series of complex questions by this council. How do we know what we can correct in the church and what we must retain? How do we distinguish between authentic tradition and accumulated elements that are not in harmony with the inner nature of the sacraments? How do we reread the texts of Scripture and use them as the basis of today's church? What systematic method would we use to examine church life to bring it authentically up to date while at the same time leaving it essentially intact as the church which Jesus Christ imagined?

As our source in considering this, we will use the inaugural speech of the Second Vatican Council, given by Pope John XXIII. Unfortunately for the listeners then, this speech was given at the conclusion of a ceremony several hours in length and in which all the participants were dressed in colorful but uncomfortable vestments and seated in the pews of a gigantic basilica, not known for its creature comforts. The ears that heard it then also didn't have the benefit of time, the perspective of the now-completely-unfolded events of the council, or leisurely exegesis of its text.

Nonetheless, the procedure used at the council can be drawn from the text of this speech and the later actions of the council fathers. Certain principles can be laid down that point us toward a method which is helpful to us today as we now approach other important pastoral concerns among the faithful. All of the following words of Pope John XXIII are taken from the English translation of this speech.

Seven Principles

Principle One:
We don't have much experience with
orderly reform so we have to invent
our method as we go along.

Reform efforts in the history of the church have by and large
not met with long-lasting success. There were, for example,
the reforms of Pope Gregory VII, whose papacy ran from
1073 to 1085. In these reforms, he sought to end abuses,
which were rampant in the church, and to free the church
from entanglement with civil government. Gregory, however,
wound up fearing for his life and living in exile from civil
government. His reforms were generally short-lived.

But even though short-lived, this papacy marked the real
beginning of reform in the church as we know it today. The
enduring contribution of this papacy flows from the fact that
Gregory admitted for the first time that abuses in the church were
widespread and that a restoration of the lifestyle of the gospels
was necessary immediately. From that time to the present,
reform of the church itself has been called for frequently.

There were also the reforms led by William of Ockham,
(d. 1347) who argued that papal authority is only acceptable
if exercised with collegiality. He also argued steadfastly for
religious liberty, that no one should be coerced to accept the
faith. William was more a spiritual leader than a "legal"
scholar, however, and his efforts did not succeed. Vatican II
eventually adopted many of his positions.

About the same time as William, there was also Marsilius
of Padua (d. 1324) who argued that the church is a spiritual
and sacramental community united by a common faith. He
pressed the principle of subsidiarity—the appropriate decen-

tralization of church authority—which was eventually adopted in this century.

There were also the reforms of many mystics and founders of religious communities. Indeed, many communities of sisters, priests, and brothers were founded for the very purpose of reform. The effects of most of these reforms was limited to a relatively small area, however, compared to the universal church.

There was also the somewhat infamous Council of Basel in 1431 which had all kinds of problems of its own and ended in fistfights on the floor as competing forces fought to gain the rostrum. This council promoted, not collegiality, but conciliarism, which basically held that councils have more authority than popes. Basel was eventually closed down by the pope and moved to Florence.

And, of course, there was the Reformation—a profound attempt at internal church reform which ended in a major cleavage of both temporal and religious leaders. This period in the sixteenth century was filled with reform and counter-reform attempts: the Fifth Lateran Council, the Lutheran movement, and the Council of Trent most notable among them.

The Council of Trent certainly regenerated the role of the bishop and had far-reaching reform effects in the entire church. And it did reform abuses that had been widespread in the church and to which the Protestant reformers had objected. But it did so mainly by countering reform with extremely tight, centrally controlled discipline. The result was not a reform of the *church* but a reform of the *people* in the church.

After the sixteenth century, there were other regional, national, and continental movements toward reform. The French Revolution, which initially did not include the reform of the church in its aim, ended in a bloody attempt at clerical and ecclesiastical reform. The reign of Pius IX seemed initially to have reform as its mission but bankrupt relationships to the temporal rulers of the time, mixed with bad advice from his Secretary of State, drove this pope into a rejection of reform and eventually, the *Syllabus of Errors,* which renounced liberalism and the modern times.

The First Vatican Council certainly had reformers present, if not successful in advancing their agenda, but it may have been the least reform-minded council in history. It was, instead, a feast of intransigence regarding the changing times and the place of the church in the modern world. It ended its work with a heavy-handed reaffirmation of the papacy as irreformable. This in the midst of an age of history concerned primarily with biological evolution, science, the emergence of psychology, and the dawn of modern communications.

Reform movements, in short, have never been far from the church or the church's leaders, even though they have rarely succeeded in their goals. But none of them has left us with a tradition of reform, a tradition of correction. We have many traditions in the church, but "appropriate correction" has not been one of them.

The popes and councils in church history have taken great pains not only to link with the past but actually to *continue* the past unchanged. At the Second Council of Nicea, for example, in 787, the following statement was published as a rationale for its approval of the use of statues and icons in churches and homes: "We subtract nothing. We add nothing. We simply preserve unsullied all that the Catholic Church holds."

That pretty well sums it up.

So the call for *aggiornamento,* or "appropriate corrections," from Pope John XXIII in the 1960s, at first glance, may have seemed only a dream—and a bad one at that!—to the Roman Curia. But somehow at this council, unlike previous ones, the council fathers avoided taking a turn against reform and actually implemented a method that resulted in real, deep, and profound corrections in the church.

The method they used, since it could not be based successfully in the tradition of the church, was based instead on their own invention, under the guidance of the Holy Spirit. All the people involved at this council, the Roman Curia, the conservative party, the progressive party, the theological and legal experts, acted out of faith. All of them sought to extol the Gospel, to take seriously Jesus' command that we "teach all nations." And, even though human pride and stubbornness sometimes crept into the proceedings, nonetheless, first and foremost, this was truly a faith-based event.

Principle Two:
The purpose of correcting the church is to
more fully live out God's superior and inscrutable
designs for the human family.
The main duty of reformers is to defend
and advance the truth about the meaning
of human life.

Our job, in short, is to guard and teach the deposit of faith, which originates with the apostles, so that what God wants for the world can unfold gracefully. Pope John said this explicitly in his inaugural speech. In this process, reformers are to have as a basis of their understanding that church doctrine "embraces the whole of the human person, composed, as persons are, of body and soul . . . the Lord has said, 'seek first the kingdom of God and God's justice'. . . (Matthew 6:33)." The word "first" is important here, he said, because it sets a priority for us. But we must not forget the rest of the verse: ". . . and all these things shall be given you."

As such, we offer the world insight and guidance in its progress, making the church extremely useful to society. But at the same time, he said, "the church must ever look to the present, to the new conditions and new forms of life introduced into the modern world which have opened new avenues to the Catholic apostolate."

Principle Three:
Maintain strong continuity with authentic tradition
but correct practices or beliefs which, although
pious, originated from local traditions imposed on
the universal church or recently added practices now
considered ancient. Likewise, hold firmly to the
central, revealed truths of the faith, but correct the
academic language used to state them.

In his inaugural speech, Pope John spoke explicitly of the permissibility and even of the necessity of restating the ancient truths of the faith in words that are more easily understood today.

The pope was clear in saying that *restating* articles of doctrine is not the same as *redefining* them. "The salient point of this council is not," he said, "a discussion of one article or another of the fundamental doctrine of the Church. . . . For this a council was not necessary."

What the world expects, he told the bishops, is a "step forward toward a doctrinal penetration and a formation of consciences in . . . conformity to the authentic doctrine which, however, should be studied and expounded through the methods of research and through the literary forms of modern thought."

Then the pope made his often quoted distinction: "The substance of the ancient doctrine of the deposit of faith is one thing, and the way in which it is presented is another." It was to the latter that he pointed the work of the bishops.

Principle Four:
Aggiornamento is based on two footings:
1. a continuous return to the sources
   of all Christian life which are the Scriptures, and
2. the adjustment of all aspects of our common life
   to the times in which we now live.

The task of *aggiornamento* proceeds employing methods of research and literary forms of modern thought, Pope John said in his inaugural speech. This is true even when these methods are applied to the Scriptures.

It is clear in this that the task of reformers is to recover the spirit and purpose of the Gospel. This is no easy task when one considers the various critical and analytical methods of study being applied to those texts today with the blessing of the church and the agreement of most serious scholars. Nonetheless, we look to our history as a guide for it is indeed the "teacher of life."

In the Scriptures we read about a community of believers forming a lifestyle out of what they remembered of Jesus Christ and how they believed he taught them to live. This lifestyle, this communal way of being together with Christ in the world, known as *koinonia,* is the church's foundation.

The author of Acts of the Apostles provides a peek into the trusting, communal nature of this lifestyle in the earliest of the Christian communities:

> The community of believers was of one heart and mind, and no one claimed that any of their possessions were their own, but they had everything in common. . . . There was no needy person among them, for those who owned property or houses would sell them, bring the proceeds of the sale, and put them at the feet of the apostles, and they were distributed to each according to his need (Acts 4:32–35).

This community of early believers grew in size, of course, so that the ideal of communism expressed here in Acts was no longer possible. Through the early preaching of Paul, Peter, and others, the church also became more geographically widespread, extending from Jerusalem along both the northern and southern shores of the Mediterranean Sea into Asia and Europe. Despite its growth, the church retained many of the characteristics of this earliest community. Believers tended to gather in one another's homes, even in the face of early persecution, and quickly grew to about 5,000 (Acts 4:4).

The Christian Scriptures provide us many clues about these early domestic meetings of the community. See, for example, Acts 17:5 where the local authorities, when searching for the Christians, came first to Jason's house, expecting them to be gathering there, which indeed they were. See also Philemon 1:2, which describes the church in Colossae meeting in the house of Philemon.

These early believers gathered for meals and to share stories of their faith. Their gatherings included the public reading of letters from other Christians, the preaching of leaders, and the collection of funds to support communities in financial need. Each congregation was called an *ekklesia*, a Greek term applied in the first century to popular assemblies in democratic municipal governments. They were mainly urban communities in the early going, most likely because missionaries could be supported only by urban centers. Little effort was made to convert rural residents and it was in this odd way that the term used to describe them, *pagani*, (which originally means "rural persons") came to refer to all pre-Christian inhabitants of the Mediterranean region.

Despite the local nature of these gatherings for breaking bread and sharing meals, the early church was also distinctly universal. Paul's use of the term *ekklesia*, for example, refers to the local church meeting in someone's home, but also in the plural form to the churches of a given region, such as the churches of Galatia (Galatians 1:2.), as well as to the worldwide church, all Christians everywhere. In the letter to Ephesians, for example, Paul refers to the church as Christ's body, "the fullness of the one who fills all things in every way (Ephesians 1:22–23).

The sacraments of baptism and Eucharist were dominant in the church then. The early church had developed a catechumenate that took baptism very seriously. Baptism then took place primarily on the Easter Vigil and was the result of rigorous formation and preparation. It was the high point of the year! Ordination to ministerial priesthood did not have the same prominence vis-a-vis baptism that it has today.

Some of the core values of the twentieth century, at least in the modern western cultures, would have been a surprise to these early Christians. They admitted slaves, for example, to baptism, but no attempt was made to emancipate them. They were comforted, presumably, by the promise of an eternal life of freedom. See, for example, the letter to Philemon where Paul sends a runaway slave home to his master after baptism but without resolving for Philemon how this slave should now be treated. For Philemon, this was an especially delicate matter, however, since the local church met in his house. In this assembly they would have read the letter from Paul to Colossians calling for, "neither Greek nor Jew . . . slave or free man, but Christ is all in all" (3:11). See also Colossians 4:1.

Likewise, women were admitted, with some rising to prominence in minor ways, but in general they were required to take only submissive roles. They were expected to come to worship with their hair covered to avoid seducing the males. Paul's instructions about women were stern (See 1 Corinthians 11:3ff).

These examples help us understand that we do not look to the church in these early years as a literal guide on how to organize ourselves today. Rather, we look to these early years in order to consider their process or method of coming to terms with their age of history, the very challenge which Pope John laid squarely before the bishops of the world in his inaugural speech.

The council examined this early history of the church carefully as it constructed its reforms, keeping in mind Pope John's instruction to examine the church with an eye to accommodating it to the "changed conditions of the times" and remaining always "predominantly pastoral."

Principle Five:
Meet errors with "the medicine of mercy
rather than that of severity. . . ."

It is better, the pope said, to demonstrate the validity of the church's teachings by extolling them and allowing people to see the light of their truth than to condemn those who disagree with us. People are wise, the pope said, and can plainly see and reject erroneous thinking on their own. For example, he said, people are aware of "those ways of life which despise God and His law, or place excessive confidence in technical progress and a well-being based exclusively on the comforts of life."

Toward this end, the church should be concerned to offer people "the goods of divine grace which . . . are the most effective safeguards and aids toward a more human life. . . ." The church, he went on, "opens the fountain of her life giving doctrine which allows [people] . . . to understand well what they really are, what their lofty dignity and their purposes are . . ."

Principle Six:
All reform must have the unity of the human family
as its ultimate goal.

It is God's will, the pope said, that all people be saved and
come to know truth. Reformers are to work toward and make
decisions that advance the "unity of humankind which is
required as a necessary foundation in order that the earthly
city may be brought to resemble the heavenly city where truth
reigns, charity is the law, and eternity is its extent."

Anything short of such a goal in church reform, also falls
short of the final prayer of Jesus for humankind, and therefore
falls short of our mission and purpose.

Principle Seven:
Reform in the church is "corrective," restoring the
Church to its true sources and purposes.

We have a strong sense of continuity with the past, not of
breaking away from it. "It is but natural," the pope said, "that
in opening this universal council we should like to look to the
past and to listen to its voices, whose echo we like to hear in the
memories and merits of" those who have gone before us. The
testimony of all this history, he said, stands before us now.

History, in a word, does not begin with us but continues
during our lifetimes. We listen to all that the people who have
come before us have had to say so that we are able to make a
meaningful comment ourselves today in this great, centuries-
long conversation about God and God's work in the world.

SUMMARY
Principle One: We don't have much experience
with orderly church reform so we have to invent our
method as we go along.

Principle Two: The purpose of correcting the church is to more fully live out God's superior and inscrutable designs for the human family. The main duty of reformers is to defend and advance the truth about the meaning of human life.

Principle Three: Maintain strong continuity with authentic tradition but not with practices or beliefs which, although pious, originated from local traditions imposed on the universal church or recently added practices considered ancient. Likewise, hold firmly to the central, revealed truths of the faith, but not the academic language used to state them.

Principle Four: Aggiornamento ("appropriate corrections") is based on two footings: (1) a continuous return to the sources of all Christian life which are the Scriptures, and (2) the adjustment of all aspects of our common life to the times in which we now live.

Principle Five: Meet errors with "the medicine of mercy rather than that of severity . . ."

Principle Six: All reform must have the unity of the human family as its ultimate goal.

Principle Seven: Reform in the church is "corrective," restoring the church to its true sources and purposes.

Five Steps in the Process of Achieving Reform in the Church Based on the Principles Set Forth Above

Step One:
Identify the area of concern: pastoral issues that affect the faith and life of the people of God . . .

The Second Vatican Council took this step through an extensive, worldwide consultation prior to its meeting. Admittedly, only Catholic males were consulted, and mainly ordained ones, but during the course of the council, a few religious women and men, laypeople, other Christians, and Jews were also involved, although none was seated as a "council father."

Throughout the council itself, new issues were identified and explored as well. A real freedom was felt during the course of the council to name the issues and deal with them openly. There were blunt speeches about the church's need for corrective measures, and about how these measures should be designed and implemented. There was no sense that speaking freely about these things would somehow undermine the authority of either the papacy or the church, a sense one sometimes gets in the years since the council ended.

Accurately identifying the needs of the Christian people is the first step toward knowing what God wants for today's church.

Step Two:
Observe these times.
Trust the progress of science,
psychology, and medicine.
Consult with professionals.

At the council, it is clear that the worldview of the church had changed in large part because the worldview of the pope had changed. Pope John was optimistic about the world. He openly disagreed with the "prophets of gloom" who foresaw only danger if the church was reformed. He and the documents of the council frequently use the word "progress," a positive term suggesting that we are moving in the direction of God's plan for the world.

Pope John was also of the view that the secular and the spiritual are radically united in their concern for the good of the human person. He was less of the view that secular and spiritual are divided—a common understanding previous to the council. He saw the church and the world in a two-way relationship where both can gain and he saw human society at the "edge of a new era"—he did not resist history as many in the Roman Curia did.

The fundamental supposition that lay beneath Pope John's view of the church's need for correction was this: Accommodate the times. Trust that the Spirit of God has not abandoned the world but is active and that the church is *in* the world.

The outcome of this, Pope John said, will be that "the church will become greater in spiritual riches and, gaining the strength of new energies therefrom, *will look to the future without fear*" (italics mine).

So, once the issues before the Christian people are identified (for example, the desire to renew the liturgy, the desire to define collegiality, the desire to clarify the church's position vis-a-vis the Jews, and so forth) then it is time to observe the times—to observe the unfolding work of God in medicine, science, psychology, the arts, and philosophy, among others. How can the living experience of today's people inform our thinking about this? How can this experience suggest solutions?

Step Three:
Propose new ideas and solutions to meet
the new needs of today's people and church.

How else will the Holy Spirit guide us but through new ideas? The very idea of calling this council came to Pope John XXIII, in his own words, "like a flash of light." Throughout the working sessions of the council—both the formal ones in the basilica and the informal ones around Rome—it was this process of paying attention to one's imagination, to one's inner voice suggesting solutions, that produced language or revisions in rites or whatever was needed. The Spirit urges us in this way.

The council fathers, for the most part, did not fear new ideas and suggestions. They even invited them from the observers who were present: lay women and men, other Christians, and non-Christians.

Ideas were, of course, proposed from which no action or correction resulted. Archbishop Hallihan of Atlanta gave a stirring speech regarding women's role in the church—but the council did not heed his call to open the diaconate to them. But the ideas themselves were welcomed and respected—and they provided the source material from which the outcomes of the council eventually flowed.

Step Four:
Return to the sources of the Christian life:
the content of the gospels and other books
of the New Testament, taken together with
the Tradition of the church.

Once the needs and issues had been identified and proposed solutions offered to update the church, the council focused itself almost immediately on this step. They turned these new ideas over in their collective minds through a process of statements, both formal and informal, that allowed all three factors to swim together:

The issues of the Christian Church,
the characteristics of the times in which we live, and
the Scriptures and Tradition of the Church.

For this, the council relied heavily upon the huge amount of work done by biblical scholars in the decades preceding it. Some of the principal theologians at the council itself were such scholars, including Cardinal Bea whose influence in many documents was significant.

One of the main forerunners of this council was an encyclical from Pius XII, *Divino Afflante Spiritu,* which opened the door on Catholic biblical scholarship. This council's work on understanding the relationship of Scripture and Tradition also advanced the place of the apostolic history of the church.

The council also relied heavily upon its theological experts. Indeed, much of the drafting of statements and documents was done by these experts (called *periti* at the council.) Many of these theologians had been considered "dangerous" by the Roman Curia before the council. But the temper of the council proceedings allowed for a free theological debate. Stories abound of attempts to silence certain theologians—but both the popes involved at the council preferred to hear the discussion.

Step Five:
Talk these matters over openly and at length.
Conduct the discussion and midrash
with brotherly and sisterly love.
Let this theological and pastoral reflection drive
careful experimentation to implement reforms,
allowing for a sensitivity to local culture.

Pope John called the bishops who sat before him on the opening day of the council to this kind of free debate, provided they have

> "serenity of mind,
> brotherly concord,
> moderation in proposals,
> dignity in discussion,
> and wisdom of deliberation."

Indeed, as the council proceedings show, debate they did. Both in the formal sessions in the council hall within the basilica as well as in other sites around the city of Rome, the participants argued and debated. They connived and planned. They used every means at their disposal to be heard and heard clearly, whether progressive or conservative. And they expressed themselves by their voting procedures. One estimate is that more than 1.5 million total ballots were cast throughout the council: that represents 1.5 million expressions of someone's mind on a matter of some kind. It's really phenomenal when one considers the unique sort of absolutely thorough consideration given to the important questions of our age by these bishops and the pope.

This final step called for talking things over in a spirit of brotherly and sisterly love and trust. It called for being moderate in proposing solutions, dignified in expressing one's point of view, peaceful—"serene," Pope John said, knowing the Holy Spirit is present, guiding the whole process.

SUMMARY

Step One: Identify the area of concern: pastoral issues that affect the faith and life of the people of God . . .

Step Two: Observe these times. Trust the progress of science, psychology, and medicine; consult with professionals

Step Three: Propose new ideas and solutions to meet the new needs of today's people.

Step Four: Return to the sources of the Christian life: the content of the Gospels and other books of the New Testament, taken together with the Tradition of the church.

Step Five: Talk these matters over openly and at length. Conduct the discussion and *midrash* with brotherly and sisterly love. Let this theological and pastoral reflection drive careful experimentation to implement reforms, allowing for a sensitivity to local culture.

Twelve Issues Now Before the Christian People Which Were Not Considered in Depth at Vatican II

Here is a list of items facing Christians today which were simply not "on the radar screen" at the council. Spend time with each of these issues using the five-step method proposed above. What outcomes emerge?

1. The Role of Women and Feminist Theology:
The council did not see this coming in 1965. The women's movement largely postdates the council. Today theology and human experience put forth an understanding of the role of women in the church and the world which the council fathers did not anticipate. How will the modern Church address this issue? How long will Catholics accept an all-male priesthood and episcopacy?

2. Liberation Theology:
For the most part, this became publicly understood after the council ended. What does it mean for the modern church? What impact will it have on the bishops and pastors? On a deeper level, what does the method of theological thinking (from below) which produced liberation theology suggest for the church?

3. Sociological Identity of Ordained Priests:
The council did not anticipate the large exodus of priests which occurred in the wake of Vatican II. Many priests are demoralized or poorly equipped for the demands of this modern church. Is this simply the fate of a "medieval" priesthood in a modern church? How should the church now care for its priests? How should priests be chosen and trained?

4. The People's Right to Eucharist:

We restored the liturgy as the central font of the Catholic life and then restricted access to it by continuing to restrict the priesthood. We now have many priestless parishes. Urban parishes are growing larger and larger. What now?

5. The Adulthood of the Laity:

The council urged a renewed spirituality and got it. Now what do we do? Now the laity also see themselves as the ministers of the church. How do we adjust? Lay people no longer obey obligingly as they once did. They form their consciences independent of the church but still consider themselves faithful Catholics.

6. Weak Faith on the Part of Many:

The council assumed that "obeying the rules" or "memorizing a catechism" was equal to "having faith" but learned too late that this isn't so. When the rules about lifestyle and behavior were relaxed, Catholics fell off in the practice of their faith. This was so because their faith was in the church rather than the Lord, who is beyond the church.

7. Birth Control:

It goes without saying that this issue has divided the laity from the hierarchy in the past several decades. What now? It has also hurt the church's image in society around the world that the church appears unwilling to address world population concerns. Can we trust the science of birth control? As with the role of women and other nonsacramental issues, have the *people* of the church just moved on and left Rome behind in the area of birth control?

8. Gay and Lesbian Catholics:

There is increasing evidence that homosexuality occurs on a regular, consistent basis in the human race. It is clear that homosexuality is present early in human development and is

———

extremely resistant to change, just as is heterosexuality. What does this new evidence mean to traditional Catholic teaching on the matter? How should gay and lesbian Catholics express their love for one another? The council did not anticipate this question.

9. Ecumenical Households:

It would not have been possible to predict that so many marriages would be ecumenical. Today in many places they represent the majority. What does this mean for family spirituality? How can children be raised in the faith when more than one faith is active in the home? How can we offer hospitality to those of other faiths at times of sacramental celebration and the need for anointing? The council refers to "other Christians" as sister and brother churches. What this means in practical terms was not worked out.

10. Divorced Catholics:

The social shame once attached to divorce, and which drove divorced Catholics into the closet, is practically gone. Divorce occurs now more often and for more appropriate reasons: addiction, abuse, violence, adultery, and the inability to give full and proper consent at the time of the wedding, among other reasons. Where is the best place for divorced Catholics to find healing and love in their lives? Is it the church courts, offering "legal" status to divorced people through the annulment process? How long will the church continue to demand of Protestants a rigorous examination of past marriage situations before allowing "valid and licit" marriages with Catholics?

11. Conservative Resurgence.

A natural outcome of such a major council is that a conservative reaction follows the initial period of reform, but a generation later. How do we keep alive the vision and spirit of the Second Vatican Council while at the same time providing a pastoral presence to those still grieving the loss of their pre-Vatican II religious system? How does the church deal with a papal staff that does not fully support the outcomes of Vatican II? Evidence of this appears in documents like *Dominus Jesu,* which was an embarrassment to most Catholics and poorly received by the world's bishops.

12. Environmental Concerns:
The council addressed many needs of the modern world but did not have this on its mind at all. Also not part of the discussion: factors affecting world population, food sources, the greenhouse effect, and the destruction of the rain forests.

Sacramental Renewal into the Future

WHEN WE REFLECT ON THE FORTY YEARS SINCE the Second Vatican Council, it provides us an opportunity to consider how the spirit of the council continues to animate the sacramental life of the church. In what ways has this renewal shaped our current sacramental preparation and practice? And how does it lead us into the future as we continue to experience the challenges of sacramental renewal?

I do not intend to offer a strict theological *examen*, but more a pastoral reflection on the past and continuing experience of the people of God. As we examine the sacramental renewal that emerged in the wake of the council, we need to situate it within the church. We need to frame it within the context of the historical and societal time and we need to view it through the prism of the council itself.

We begin by acknowledging that the church is a communal endeavor. Jesus did not call *an* apostle, rather he called apostles. Although we may have individual pieties and spiritualities, we go to God *together.* We are the church because we worship together. We express who we are as the community of believers, the church, through our rituals, our spiritual life. Thus, when our rituals are altered or our sacramental experience is changed, it creates a major tremor among the faithful—and the shock waves continue yet.

The sessions of the Second Vatican Council were convened between October 1962, and December 1965. Pope John XXIII, as well as the bishops and cardinals who gathered for the council, trusted and believed that the Holy Spirit was in their midst. Almost miraculously, over 2,000 delegates from around the globe were able to come to virtual consensus as they voted. Rather than throwing things out, their work illuminated our traditions. Although the renewal of the sacraments occurred outside the council itself, this renewal was mandated by the council. And the mandate called for renewal of all seven sacraments, not just a select few.

Prior to 1974, the most recent sacramental reform in the church had occurred during the papacy of Pius X (1903–1914), when the age for children to come to First Eucharist was lowered to seven years of age. By 1974, sixty years after Pius X, the renewal of all seven sacraments had been written, but the renewal itself was far from complete.

The Rite of Christian Initiation of Adults

It is impossible to discuss sacramental renewal without first acknowledging the importance and impact of the Rite of Christian Initiation of Adults—or the R.C.I.A. as it has come to be known. The restoration of the catechumenate was passed on the bishops' vote of 2,165 yes, 9 no, and 1 null. A provisional ritual was subsequently distributed in 1966, and then a second draft was distributed in 1969.

In 1972 the church promulgated the *Order of Christian Initiation of Adults.* The United States bishops followed in 1986 with additions, national statutes, and a national plan for implementation. In September 1988, the church required mandatory implementation of the Rite of Christian Initiation of Adults. The document has since had an incredible impact on the way we prepare for, experience, and understand the sacraments of initiation. It has inspired the church to:

- Celebrate the Easter sacraments together at the Easter Vigil.
- Restore the order of the sacraments of initiation— Baptism, Confirmation, then Eucharist.
- Recognize that faith is a journey and conversion is on-going.
- Affirm the essential role of the community of believers.
- Articulate that there is one baptism in Jesus Christ.
- Support reflection on the Sunday readings of the *Lectionary* as the source of transformational catechesis.

Challenges for the Future

The R.C.I.A. is the norm against which we hold all sacramental preparation. It continues to prompt us to examine our past and current practices, and it forces us to see with new eyes how the sacraments of initiation are interrelated. We can no longer approach baptism, confirmation, and Eucharist as singular or isolated sacraments.

- Adaptation and application of the R.C.I.A. to children of catechetical age has yet to become widespread, consistent, and true to the rite.

- The R.C.I.A. continues to contradict policies and practices around the sacrament of confirmation.
- The integrity of the rites of the R.C.I.A. process must be preserved.

Baptism

Prior to renewal, baptism was viewed by the faithful as a private event for "this" baby. We lacked an appreciation that all sacraments are public events—the public expressions of the church. The faith of the faithful gathered was not recognized as essential. We had little appreciation of God's care for the unbaptized and a narrow view of the role of parents and godparents.

The renewal illumined our understanding and experience of Baptism in many ways:

- The celebration of baptism was brought into the Sabbath Eucharist, emphasizing the public and communal nature of the sacrament. This change helped to remind the assembly of their own baptismal call, and of their obligation to help form these new members in the faith.
- The council affirmed that parents are the first and primary religious educators of their children. And because our ritual speaks our belief, parents were now allowed to hold their child at baptism. (Prior to this time, parents were seen as unworthy and only the sponsor was allowed to hold the child.)
- The church spoke clearly that God has loved each child from the very first moment of being.
- The church no longer rebaptized Christians who were becoming Catholic.

- The Rite of Christian Initiation of Adults was promulgated.

Challenges for the Future

Baptism and our understanding of "baptismal call" are essential to the continuing sacramental life of the church. We cannot take lightly our practices and teachings around the sacrament of baptism—it is the gateway through which all enter. We need to take the challenges below seriously:

- The symbols and rituals of baptism need to shout our belief. We need to get serious about using immersion pools and oil in abundance. Meager symbols do not speak of the incredible power of baptism, nor of a generous God.
- Many Catholics still do not comprehend what "baptismal call" means, and many who may know do not embrace it.
- We need to solve the logistic problems that keep parishes from baptizing within the Sabbath Eucharistic. The entire assembly needs to be renewed by this experience on a regular basis.
- Efforts regarding preparation for baptism need to be scrutinized and evaluated. Does our vision extend beyond the day of baptism?

Confirmation

Prior to renewal, our perception of confirmation was that it was a sacrament totally separate from baptism. Through this sacrament we saw ourselves commissioned as "soldiers of

Christ." We were allowed to select a confirmation sponsor and a confirmation name—a saint's name. In many instances, confirmation signaled the conclusion of religious education, or "graduation."

In the renewal of Confirmation we find:

- Confirmation is seen as the second sacrament of the sacraments of initiation—a step in the process toward full initiation.
- The connection with baptism is strongly emphasized—candidates are encouraged to keep their baptismal sponsor as well as their baptismal name.
- Rather than a rite of maturity or commitment, confirmation confirms our baptism and affirms the action of the Holy Spirit in our lives.

Challenges for the Future

Mention the word "confirmation" and you can ignite a heated discussion. Still, forty years after Vatican II, and more than thirty years since the renewal of the sacrament, many of the mandates regarding confirmation have been given little serious effort. With this sacrament, the challenges impact many in the church.

- The age for confirmation as defined in canon law (canon 891) remains seven years of age. However, it is within each local bishop's purview to designate an age policy for his particular diocese. The question remains: Should age be the determiner of readiness for any sacrament?
- In the liturgical renewal of the council, the church was directed to restore the order of the sacraments of initiation. In fact, many

bishops have mandated that confirmation be restored to its original order—that is, prior to Eucharist. Still, many have not.

• Where adolescent confirmation is the policy, it often becomes the sacrament of exit from church programs, perhaps from worship. When we make requirements for confirmation so stringent, youngsters may logically conclude that once all is completed, they graduate from religious education.

• In placing unrealistic requirements on confirmation preparation, we have prompted many young people to opt out of the sacrament. The numbers of those who remain unconfirmed is staggering.

• We have mistakenly offered confirmation as a sacrament of maturity, a ritual of passage. In fact, it is a sacrament of initiation—a beginning. How do we repair this?

• In many places, confirmation preparation, for whatever age, is more related to a classroom religion class than to initiatory catechesis. Liturgical catechesis is lost in the shuffle and a spiritual focus is often lacking.

• Confirmation policies are often at odds with the R.C.I.A. For example, within the R.C.I.A., unbaptized children of catechetical age are baptized, confirmed, and receive Eucharist at the same event. Meanwhile, their neighbor who is a lifelong Catholic may be required by diocesan policy to wait until high school for confirmation.

Eucharist

In the years prior to Vatican II, we saw the consecrated bread, the Eucharist—the body of Christ—as separate from the Mass. Our attention was primarily on the actions and words of consecration. The prayer of the Eucharist was in Latin and the priest had his back to the people. For the most part, the congregation was a silent observer. Altar boys, as we referred to them then, were the only ones in the sanctuary other than the priest.

As the renewal began to enter parish life, changes around the celebration of the Eucharist were sometimes obvious physical changes, and at other times more subtle.

- The altar was turned around to face the people.
- The Eucharist was prayed in the vernacular of the people—for most Americans this meant in English.
- Liturgical ministries were expanded to include lectors and readers, Eucharistic ministers of communion, ministers of hospitality, altar servers (including girls), ministers of music, and lay presiders.
- Liturgical ministries were open to lay men and women, young and old.
- Lay people shared in parish liturgical planning.
- The congregation became known as the assembly and began to sing and participate in musical prayer forms. Gradually such music was sung in the language of the people, and became reflective of their varied ethnic cultures.
- As frequent communion was encouraged, communion for the faithful came to include both sacred species. Not only do communicants begin taking Jesus' body in their hands, but they also share in the cup.

- Men and women are commissioned as lay ministers of communion.
- The three-year cycle of readings for the *Lectionary* has provided broad exposure to the scriptures. And, with the exception of the gospel, the scriptures are often proclaimed by lay people.
- The experience of hearing the scriptures proclaimed in the midst of the assembly is given great emphasis. The communal hearing of the scriptural proclamations acknowledges the power of the Holy Spirit in the midst of the people. It further speaks of the Spirit's power to transform their lives through those scriptures. This is indeed a change from the days when individuals read the scriptures from a page in a missalette.
- The homily has become a vehicle for breaking open the scriptures and allowing God's word to be transformational in people's lives.
- The assembly's responsibility for prayers, acclamations, and responses within the Mass is articulated. Clearly, full and active participation is expected.
- The general intercessions have truly become the prayer of the faithful. The assembly hears these communal prayers in their own language, and offers their assent.
- In what had previously been a silent time, the greeting of peace moves people to speak to one another in Christ's own words, "Peace be with you."
- The liturgical feasts and seasons of the church receive heightened recognition in prayer and music, as well as in liturgical environments.
- Even the environment and architecture has come to speak of liturgical reform. Churches provide spaces where people gather and are welcomed, as well as

places where parishioners can meet and greet one another before or after Mass. Even the way the church space is configured reflects the importance of the assembly. Of course, the faithful are meant to see the altar and the sanctuary, but they are intended to see one another as well. After all, they are the one body of Jesus Christ.

Overall, a great deal of the liturgical reform of the council was focused on the celebration of the Eucharist. The council reminded us that the Eucharist is the central event in the life of the church. It is the focus toward which all parish efforts are aimed. As such, the Eucharist calls for the full and active participation of all the assembly.

Challenges for the Future

Priest shortages have become critical in many areas. How will this affect the availability of Sabbath Eucharist?

- Can Word-Communion services satisfy the faithful's desire for the full celebration of the Eucharist?
- Will church communities be able to sustain their identity and sense of being one body in Christ without regularly gathering at Eucharist?
- Intercommunion remains one of the major remaining barriers to ecumenical efforts of the past forty years.
- The Eucharist is the center of Catholic life. We are a Eucharistic people. How will we remain so in the years ahead?

Reconciliation

As the church entered the decade of the sixties, the faithful had already begun to celebrate the sacrament of penance less often. The societal times were riddled with revolution, rebellion, and sexual freedom. People were antiwar, antigovernment, anti-institution, and antiauthority. As the decade progressed, these attitudes only increased. These were not times when the masses—even Catholics—were searching their souls, informing their conscience, or acknowledging their sinfulness. For reasons that were probably religious but also influenced by the times, the sacrament of penance was being embraced less and less, even by many faithful Catholics.

Over many decades, we had become a church that was extremely legalistic regarding sin. For many years our focus was on confessing an itemized listing of our sins along with the number of offences. In fact, we commonly referred to the sacrament as "confession." Our sense of sin was that it was a private offense, and that it was between the individual and God. Confession was a private matter, and so was sin.

One aspect of the renewal of the sacrament of penance involved some physical change. No longer was the confessional the site of all sacramental forgiveness. The celebration of the sacrament was brought into the church worship space.

The renewal also involved some major changes in the ritual itself. Rather than the familiar confessional formula, "Bless me father, for I have sinned, . . ." now there were three forms of the sacrament of reconciliation—as it came to be known. *Form One* is meant to be celebrated in a space designated for celebrating the sacrament rather than in a confessional, involves only the individual penitent and the confessor, or priest. *Form Two* provides for several (or more) penitents in a communal setting, but still allows for individual absolution. *Form Three* also provides for several penitents but allows for general absolution. All of these forms include the sharing of scripture, a confession of sinfulness, as well as a ritual gesture of absolution.

The renewal involved some major changes in understanding and attitudes as well:

- The sacrament has come to be recognized as an authentic personal and communal prayer form.
- We focus on God's gracious mercy and forgiveness rather than our list of sins. We begin to see that God's forgiveness is mediated to us in many ways— not all sacramental. And we are more aware that God will *always* forgive us—all we need to do is ask.
- As a church we are growing in our recognition of communal sin and our shared guilt.
- Communal rites have helped us realize that sin is not just between the individual and God, and that a sacrament is a public, not a private event.
- Gradually we are coming to understand that sacramental forgiveness has a place in the rhythms of life, as well as in the liturgical seasons of the church year.
- Our understanding of sin has deepened. The renewal promoted individual responsibility for conscience formation. We are coming to know that what is in our heart—our intention—is more important than what is on the list of recognized sins. We are being encouraged to discern what truly underlies our sinful actions, and to recognize the temptations in our lives. We are becoming more aware of societal sins and our culpability in those.

Challenges for the Future

Many of the factors that influenced the sacrament of reconciliation prior to Vatican II continue today.

Furthermore, new factors have come on the scene, some of which are connected to other challenges that the church now faces.

- The number of Catholics who participate in the sacrament of reconciliation continues to decline.
- We still do not acknowledge one of the most inspiring teachings of the council— that the Eucharist is the primary source of reconciliation in the church.
- How will the declining number of ordained ministers affect the ability of local churches to provide sacramental absolution?
- In light of recent scandals within the church, how will we inspire a standard of morality that can be a beacon for all?

Anointing of the Sick

Prior to Vatican II, few Catholics had ever witnessed, much less experienced, what was then commonly referred to as "extreme unction." Our view was that, at best, this was a person's last confession. At worst, it was some vague anointing that occurred at the time of death or immediately thereafter.

As with the other sacraments, the renewal of this sacrament brought its celebration into the communal realm. As we became more consistent in referring to it as "Anointing of the Sick," our words spoke the reality.

- Anointing of the Sick has become integrated into the public prayer life of the church. This allows the assembly to pray with and for those in need of healing.
- We recognize that those who desire this sacrament are not only the dying, but also the chronically ill,

the critically ill, the very elderly, and the very young.

• The faithful have come to understand that sacramental prayer can sanctify suffering, illness, and death, not only for the individual, but also for their loved ones. This has become a powerful example to all believers.

• As a church, we have come to realize that Jesus has shared the power to heal with us all. We cannot help but be touched by the awesome healing power of prayer—in particular the prayer of the community.

Challenges for the Future

As with other areas of the sacramental life of the Church, the continuing shortage of ordained ministers will likely impact this sacrament as well.

• Lay people are increasingly involved in ministry to the hospitalized, the homebound, and the ill. Still, an ordained priest is the minister of the sacrament of anointing.

• As the population ages and the number of elderly and infirm increases, the need for anointing will increase as well.

• As the number of Catholic hospitals declines, the need for Catholic chaplains continues to grow. Permanent deacons and lay people may fill this need, but still an ordained priest is the minister of anointing.

Matrimony

Anyone who was married in the Catholic Church prior to the sacramental renewal can tell of a ceremony over which they had no say. They simply fulfilled the marriage preparation requirements—if there were any—and showed up for a liturgical event which may have had little meaning for them, since they had nothing to do with its preparation. No wonder the focus was on the trappings, the wedding paraphernalia, and the reception.

In the sacramental renewal, which flowed out of the council, even Matrimony received its share of attention.

- We articulated the specific roles of the individuals involved in the liturgical event of matrimony. The bride and groom are the ministers of the sacrament; the priest is their witness.
- Couples are included in the planning of the ceremony. They may select readings and music, and they may make choices about other liturgical possibilities, such as candle lighting, etc. Additionally, the couple may invite family or friends to serve in the liturgical ministries of hospitality, music, reading, and distributing communion.
- Catholics can be married in other Christian churches, often with Catholic clergy participating.
- There are more stringent requirements for marriage preparation.
- As a part of the restoration of the order of permanent deacon, permanent deacons were given faculties to witness marriages.

Challenges for the Future

In many instances, the challenges that face the sacrament of matrimony remain the same as they have been.

- How to help couples comprehend the meaning of a sacramental marriage.
- How to provide marriage preparation that is effective.
- How to support marriage and family within parish life.
- How to implement preparation requirements that are reasonable and possible for the couple to fulfill.
- How to maintain the liturgical integrity of the sacrament of matrimony while still allowing a couple to participate in the planning and celebration.

Holy Orders

The easiest way to consider the sacrament of Holy Orders prior to the renewal is to see it through the eyes of the faithful in the pews. The expectation was that "Father" should be all things to all people—available at a moment's notice for whatever need, able to stretch limited financial resources to be a theologian, a scripture scholar, a dynamic preacher, and most importantly, a man who required no day off and could manage to get thirty hours of availability into every twenty-four-hour day.

In the wake of renewal, many of the changes that affected the ordained went on behind the scenes. But, even though those in the pews probably saw few changes, attitudes and perceptions began to change.

- The council restored the ancient order of the permanent deaconate, which brought laymen into ordained ministry. Deacons receive faculties to preach and baptize, and they can preside at marriages and funerals, as well. In keeping with historical tradition, the ministry of the permanent deaconate is service.

• The council gave local bishops more authority to govern and oversee their dioceses.

• The documents articulate the varied roles of the ordained more clearly: the pope and bishops are ordained as chief teachers; the priest is ordained as leader of worship; the deacon is ordained to service.

• As parishes increase in size, pastors have recruited parish staffs of religious and lay professionals who can share parish ministries.

• The church took note of the needs of the ordained and now requires continuing education for priests and encourages priests to establish support groups among their peers.

Challenges for the Future

There are numerous issues that continue to swirl around the sacrament of Holy Orders and ordination. All are complex, and many are interrelated.

• Scandals involving sexual abuse and miscon-duct have rocked the church.

• The declining numbers of ordained have already impacted today's parishes.

• The influx of foreign-born clergy has helped to alleviate priest shortages but has presented new difficulties emerging from cultural differences.

• The discussion around allowing priests to marry will not go away.

- In many ways, the faithful now have more realistic expectations of priests. However, the institutional church continues to put unrealistic demands on their priests, such as serving more than one parish, becoming sacramental functionaries as they travel from parish to parish each weekend, and later retirement ages.
- In the church's eager desire for vocations to the priesthood, standards for ordination may be compromised.
- The conversation around women and ordination refuses to be silenced. It has been said that there is no shortage of vocations, we just don't ordain them all.

Conclusion

Obviously, the work begun at the Second Vatican Council is not yet completed. Many challenges still remain. As far-reaching as sacramental renewal has been, it has not altered our core beliefs. Nevertheless, our understanding and our experience of the sacraments have changed in significant ways. As a church, we value our sacramental life. It is these rituals—the sacramental expressions of the church—that speak our belief.

As we believe the Holy Spirit inspired those gathered at the council, we believe the Spirit remains with the church. So, pack your bags, let the Holy Spirit be your guide, and set your sights on continuing the journey into the future with the church.

Speak Out for the Sake of the Church

OH, IT WAS A VERY CATHOLIC (WITH A SMALL C) crowd that showed up at the opening session of Vatican II, almost forty years ago. Most of that bunch (some two thousand five hundred of the world's bishops) were very unsure of what they were there for, but they might have found a clue by looking around them. (Sometimes, as that great philosopher Yogi Berra once said, you can see a lot just by looking.) Pittsburgh saw Pernambuco, Manhattan looked at Madagascar, Raleigh ogled Riobamba, and Hyderabad regarded Hiroshima—yellow faces and black faces and brown faces and ruddy faces, but hardly any really white faces. They might have realized on that day that the church might well become in intention what it already was in fact: more catholic, less Roman.

But few knew that, then, at the beginning. The Roman Curia, still living in a Renaissance court, had put its mark on the preconciliar period, so much so that some U.S. bishops thought they were there for only one purpose: to rubber stamp Rome's absolutist, legalistic view of the church—then go home in three or four weeks. After only a day or two, however (and then for the rest of that enchanted autumn), they could hardly believe their ears.

They heard some of the church's most senior cardinals speaking more like Nathan Hale or Patrick Henry than Torquemada, speaking about the church's need for selfless service, not the institution's own needs. They heard a perceptive cardinal from Bologna telling them the church didn't have all the answers, that it was on a wandering, sweaty, pilgrim-march through history. They heard another learned cardinal from the Roman Curia telling them that their scholars and preachers had to get back to the church's Scriptural and historic roots. They heard an enlightened archbishop from Belgium telling them about the dangers of triumphalism and juridicism and clericalism, and a humble archbishop from Brazil asking them to sell their diamond and ruby encrusted chalices and give them to the poor. They heard an auxiliary bishop from Paris telling them that Catholic France had lost the working class; a Dutch missionary bishop from Tanganyika telling them that the age of colonialism was over, even and especially for the church; and a bishop from Bora Bora telling them that his people understood the parables of Jesus, but didn't understand (or much care about) papal infallibility.

T.D. Roberts, the retired archbishop of Bombay, told me at the time, "They were saying things I'd always thought, but never dared utter." That gave him, and most of his confreres, the courage to speak out as they never had before, without fear, something that probably had no place in the church when it was born—at the first Pentecost. Only later, when the church started becoming more of an empire than a family did the sycophantic church emerge.

As for the pope, Angelo Giuseppe Roncalli, John XXIII, well, they saw a jolly fellow who did not have much truck with sycophants, or believe in condemning the world, or crying havoc over it, but, rather, in loving it and trying to make it a better place for his nieces and nephews. He didn't want to keep the barque of Peter in dry dock much longer. "Scrape the barnacles of history off the bottom of this ship," he said in effect, "and let's set sail and get the saving message of salvation out on to the seas of the world." And then good Pope John got out of the way. He didn't remain inside the temporary bleachers they'd erected under the dome of St. Peter's, but retired to his apartment, to watch the proceedings on closed-circuit TV in private, and pray for the descent of the Holy Spirit on his council.

Soon the bishops realized they were gathered in a sure enough parliamentary proceeding—it was only the twentieth such council of the church in twenty centuries, and it was certainly the most wide-ranging of them all (except, possibly, the council of Trent). They were there not to hear what the Holy Father thought, but to tell him—and one another— what *they* thought. Encouraged by good Pope John, who had nothing to fear from his bishops speaking frankly, they exercised something quite common in the early church, but quite rare in the church of Pius X, and Pius XI, and Pius XII. It is what we call in America . . . freedom of speech.

I ATTRIBUTE MUCH of the success of the council to this plain talk (even though it was in Latin). And to the fact that the people of God had a chance to eavesdrop on what the fathers of the council were saying and doing. The Curia had decreed that the council be closed to the press, but we members of the press who were there found ways to open it up. This made it possible for the people of God not only to know what was happening inside the council, but to applaud

---

137

the bishops, too. Even *Time* magazine started cheering for the *aggiornamento* of Pope John XXIII. Archbishop Roberts (who had come to my home for dinner one night and stayed two years) told me he could see copies of *Time* being passed up and down the temporary bleachers each Tuesday. The positive press reaction told the bishops they were on the right track, and they became even bolder reformers. They even surprised themselves.

I confess feeling a humble pride in this dynamic. I had no doubt that I was being used by the Holy Spirit (I did my part, working eighteen hours a day) by playing a role in breaking down a major myth, the myth that the pope and the bishops got their instructions directly from on high. As the council unfolded, we could all see how the church leadership made its decisions. The council was just like any session of the U.S. Congress, or the British Parliament: it got things done through vigorous, often heated, man-to-man debate, some excellent staff work, and a few backroom deals besides. Almost overnight, our view of the church as a pyramid with its peak reaching all the way to heaven came tumbling down. All of a sudden, everything started making more sense— as it should, in a secular world where there were few, if any secrets.

I don't know how many were aware then of the larger import of what was happening. I was there, and I didn't understand as fully then as I do now. I see now, in retrospect, what happened at Vatican II. Because the bishops were able to speak their minds, and because they received a good deal of encouragement from the people of God, they were able to write a bold new charter for the church—to make it more democratic, more pluralistic, more free, more human, more humble in the face of history.

I submit that, among the things *we* can do, the first thing we can do (after a little prayer and some serious thought) is to *speak out*—first to our colleagues, and then to anyone who will listen to us.

You say you don't have the right? Yes, you do. But you will get the message across better if you call it a duty. If we believe in the message of the Gospel, then we have a duty to start speaking frankly. Why? Because it is our church? Well, theoretically yes. The journalist John Cogley summed up the principal message of Vatican II in one of his "Poems on Postcards" that were published regularly in *America* magazine during Vatican II.

> Who Is the Church?
> Who?
> You.

I WOULD LIKE TO CUT now to the figure of the most complex and, therefore, one of the most exasperating, popes in history, Karol Wojtyla, Pope John Paul II. In 1980, during his first visit to the United States as pope, I did a front-page story in the *New York Times* on his appearance in Madison Square Garden before almost twenty thousand teenagers. He came riding into the arena standing in an open jeep, as several high-school bands banged out the theme from "Rocky," bouncing on the balls of his feet, and giving them a smiling sign of approval, with his thumbs up. When he finally got to the microphone, he expressed his awe at the kids' exuberance, and he let them sport with them. Mischievously, they wouldn't let him speak, taking turns, one section after another, with organized cheers, sometimes adapting those cheers to him.

> Rack 'em up, stack 'em up.
> Break 'em in two.
> Holy Father, we're for you.

139

"Wu, wu, wu," he said, finally, after eighteen minutes of organized chaos. A charismatic moment. "Wu wu wu" is Polish for "wow wow wow." I could feel the good will in the Garden that day. I had the sense that this pope would do anything to understand (and be understood) by the kids. And that the kids would have done anything for him, because if he really meant that he liked hanging out with the charismatic church (as opposed to the hierarchical church), then this was a church they could swing with.

Even *I* liked him that day, I who was spoiled by John XXIII, and maybe a little resentful of anyone who couldn't match him. John XXIII had chatted with me for forty minutes one day in August before the first session of the council, helping me understand that he wanted his council to bring people together and not foster dumb divisions based on illusory ideologies. I remember our talking about the Cold War, fostered in part by Pius XI and Pius XII, and his telling me he didn't want any more Cold War. It was a lot like the Crusades, he said, and as a historian, he knew those battles against the evil empire of Islam were at the beginning a way of dealing with the unemployment problem in France, and then, toward the end, a way of enriching the papacy.

But soon, I didn't much like John Paul II. He went to Chicago after a few days in New York, and lectured the U.S. bishops—about an issue that most of them thought irrelevant, birth control! He jetted on down to Washington, DC and when Sister Teresa Kane stood up to him and asked him to consider the ordination of women, he put her down with a simplistic and probably scripted remark, telling her that "the Blessed Virgin wasn't ordained." In fact, in the early church, no one was ordained, and I was hugely disappointed that this two hundred sixty-third successor of Peter knew so little history.

He knew more about contemporary politics, and I saw greatness in him when he made those early appearances in

Poland before crowds of a million or more living under the Communist yoke crying out that they wanted God. He helped trigger a people's revolution that overthrew Communism throughout Eastern Europe without firing a shot. He was all for freedom in Poland and Estonia and Latvia, in Hungary and Rumania and Czechoslovakia. But he forgot about espousing freedom in the church. Through the years, he became a more truculent version of Pius XII, soliciting his Wednesday audiences with ideas on everything he knew almost nothing about. He spent a whole year's worth of Wednesday audiences advising married couples about sex.

He soon grew bored with trying to reform the Roman Curia, and decided the world's Catholics needed to see him, so he became Alitalia's most frequent flyer, and started drawing the biggest crowds in the history of the planet. A million or more in Puebla, Mexico. Five million in Manila. With that smiling Slavic face, looking a lot like Don Shula, he became a media icon. But underneath that smile, he was always thinking of ways to punish people (particularly theologians like Hans Küng) who didn't agree with his Polish take on the church. His church, not Christ's church, or the people's church.

During a nine-day visit to Costa Rica, Panama, El Salvador, Guatemala, Honduras, Belize and Haiti in March of 1983, he said he didn't want the folks in Central America to think of themselves as "a people's church"—even though that is very close to what he told the people of Poland only a few years before.

I could cite chapter and verse on Papa Wojtyla's almost twenty-three years as pope, and about the oceans of pious words he has uttered in almost every nation on earth. I could also tell you how much admiration I have for him. He has not been in perfect health since he was run over by a truck at age nineteen and left for dead in a ditch. But here he is, now, with

Parkinson's, but, at eighty-two, still a battler. He has hung in there for twenty-three rounds—when lesser fighters would have thrown in the towel after the fifth, or the tenth, or the fourteenth, round. According to his lights, he has given all he could for the church, and then some.

He could have given so much more if he had only learned to listen. I know one bishop from Canada who was at lunch one day with the pope. He told the pope that his part of Western Canada needed more priests; they ought to talk, he said, about the ordination of married men. The pope pretended he didn't hear. Later, the bishop brought up the subject again. This angered the pope. With his knife clenched in one hand and his fork in the other, he slammed his fists down on the table. *Deus providebit!* he screamed. *Deus providebit.* "God will provide." End of discussion.

ACCORDING TO THE COUNCIL'S charter, the church ought to be more like a family than a multinational corporation, and you might expect free discussion around that family's dinner table. You do not find much free discussion at this pope's *pranso*. I wonder if you can find it today at the dinner table of Cardinal Law in Boston or Cardinal Egan in New York. If the church is a loving family, where—in which dioceses—do we find a free, fearless exchange between a bishop and his people, or even between a bishop and his priests? A family that doesn't talk—freely—is a dysfunctional family. We need bishops who, like good fathers, can listen, or, as we have been taught to look upon them, like Good Shepherds who can say, "I know mine and mine know me." They cannot know their people if their people can never talk with them, one on one.

Forgive me, but I became a bit jaundiced when I got back on the religion beat in 1999, and started taking a closer look at Catholicism around the world, and in Rome. Today's

Rome is so different than the Rome of Vatican II. At Vatican II, the theologians and the bishops were all excited about taking the Gospel into new places and new marketplaces. In the most vital parts of today's church, in the so-called movements like Communion and Liberation, the young men talk about restoring the preconciliar church, and putting the Mass back in Latin. Inside the Curia, the monsignori speak in bored tones about *la chiesa stessa,* the church itself (meaning themselves) and about the rest of the Catholics in the world whose duty is to pray, pay and . . . shut up, while their answer machine churns out more answers than there are questions.

I have seen a good many documents over the pope's signature that tend more and more to bring power back to the so-called center of Christendom, but his actions often conflict with his words. Am I saying the Holy Father doesn't know what he is signing? or doesn't care? or that he thinks consistency is the hobgoblin of little minds? I frankly do not know the answer because the pope's gatekeepers, unlike Pope John's, bar me from the sacred presence. I would like to ask the pope some key questions—about a hundred and one questions.

Last year, John Paul II approved written cautions from the Holy Office about the dangers of interreligious dialogue. Then he proceeded to continue doing what he has done for most of this papacy—he has engaged in interreligious dialogue with the leaders of every known religion on earth. He said he authorized but did not sign the Holy Office document called *Dominus Iesus*, which asserted that the Roman Catholic Church was the only portal to salvation. Then, when criticism rained down on Rome from every corner of the globe, the pope spent several weeks trying to explain *Dominus Iesus* away. In 1996, John Paul gave a gold pectoral cross to George Carey, the Anglican Archbishop of Canterbury, and silver pectoral crosses to Carey's associate bishops. A pectoral cross is the symbol of a bishop's office. Two years later, Cardinal Ratzinger not only denied the validity of Anglican orders, but said the judgment (dating all the way back to Pope Leo XIII) was infallible. In fact, John Paul's entire papacy has been a series of these puzzling contradictions. His words say one thing, his actions another.

THE ALL-TIME CONTRADICTORY MOVE was the beatification on September 3, 2001, of two popes, John XXIII, good Pope John, and Pius IX, Pio Nono. It was a strange linkage, of the anachronistic and the prophetic. Pius IX wrote the *Syllabus of Errors*, a catalogue of all the so-called modern heresies, including religious liberty, which he said was a "delirium." Less than a century later, John XXIII was pushing the council's decree on religious liberty.

To shore up his temporal power in what was then the Papal States, Pius IX forced the Fathers of Vatican I to sign a decree that declared him infallible, but the ink was hardly dry on those signatures when Garibaldi marched in and seized the Papal States. John XXIII used to joke about his infallibility. "I think it will rain today," he told his secretary, Monsignor Capovilla. "Are you sure about that?" asked Capovilla, playing the straight man. "Well, maybe it won't rain," said Papa Roncalli. "I'm not infallible, you know."

Piux IX didn't give a damn about Protestants. John XXIII welcomed them to choice seats at his council, and called them separated brethren. Pius IX had the walls of the Rome ghetto rebuilt, and then ordered the Jews to get back in there. John XXIII received Jews from all over the world and said to each of them, "I am Joseph your brother."

Pius IX lived in a Rome where Jewish babies were baptized in secret and taken away from their families. He himself adopted one of them. By contrast, John XXIII refused to baptize a young Jew from Venice, and then, when the young man insisted, John baptized him and told him to go back to Venice and tell no one, and remain attached to the community of his forbears, "because, by becoming a Catholic, you do not become any less of a Jew."

And now, on September 3, 2001, John Paul was lifting both Pio Nono and John XXIII up the ranks of the Blesseds, not many months after a solemn ceremony during the Jubilee Year when he had begged God's pardon for a church that had employed "violence (against Jews) in the cause of truth."

But the people who were in St. Peter's Square on September 3 had *their* say, putting their veto on John Paul by exercising a form of public opinion in the church that went all the way back to the earliest days of the Roman church, when saints were made by the acclamation of the people. When, during his homily, John Paul II announced the name of Pope John, a thunderous applause broke across the Square in successive waves up to the steps in front of the basilica, and then crashed into the newly washed marble of the cathedral. The pope sat there and waited patiently for the sound waves to subside.

Then he pronounced the name of Pio Nono.

Silence, like the silence that precedes an earthquake. Equal tapestries bearing the likeness of John and Pius hung from the balustrade, same size, same colors, same glory. But these former popes were not on a par with the people's sense of the faith. "The popular vote," wrote Giancarlo Zizola, who has been covering the Vatican longer than almost anyone, "fell in favor of Pope John's gentle model of Petrine service over the pessimistic, authoritarian, anathematizing model of Pius IX. The people had voted. They loved the pope, but they didn't love his throne. That silence had made it clear: the only acceptable future for the papacy was the bare, stripped down, brotherly authority of John XXIII."

It may have taken a while for that message to sink in. Some members of the Roman Curia haven't seemed to get it.

Only recently, I have read headlines from various news services on the Internet that tell me the anathematizing habits of the papacy under Pio Nono die hard in the Roman Curia.

Zenit: POPE SAYS ACADEMIC FREEDOM SELF-DEFEATING FOR THEOLOGIANS

Associated Press: BISHOP IN MEXICO TOLD TO STOP ORDAINING INDIANS

Zenit: EURO PARLIAMENTARIANS ASSAIL PAPAL ADDRESS ON DIVORCE

These negative news bulletins aren't the fault of John Paul II, who is too feeble these days to correct anything but the most egregious gaffes that are cooked up in the Roman Curia. But, now, at last, and finally, I think he is trying to move the Curia in a new direction. As I reported earlier, the pope is beginning to get it. On January 18, 2002, the Holy Father gave a talk to members of the Holy Office that was obviously not drafted (as is usual) by someone in the Holy Office, for it criticized the Holy Office. He said he could see that the Holy Office was encountering "difficulties of reception."

If you unpack this bit of Vatican-speak, you could conclude that the pope was telling Ratzinger and company that they didn't understand the mass media; they didn't act as if they knew what century they were living in; and they didn't know how to translate the Gospel in terms their contemporaries can comprehend. You may laugh, but I have to point out that this is the first time in his papacy that John Paul II has averted to the ancient doctrine of reception. It's a line that has a lot to do with public opinion in the church, something that Pius XII once pointed out is necessary to the health of the church.

What is the doctrine of reception? There's a common misperception among many members of the press (and even among some Catholics), that the pope and his priests (often called "the hierarchy") tell the faithful what to believe and that the faithful gulp and say, "Okay, if you say so."

Theologically and historically, the reality is (or ought to be) just the opposite: the hierarchy's role is to confirm what the people believe. In 1950, when Pius XII was considering a rare, *ex cathedra* statement on the Assumption of the Blessed Virgin Mary into heaven, he first polled all the bishops in the world and asked them what their people believed regarding Mary's "ascension into heaven, body and soul." Only after he got the results of that poll did he go ahead and declare that the Assumption was "of faith." He didn't say Christians had to believe it. He said this is what Christians believe.

Or we can cite the birth control controversy of the 1960s, when a majority of Catholics did not receive the encyclical, *Humanae Vitae*, Pope Paul VI's ban on contraception. Neither did roughly a third of the world's bishops, according to a meticulous study by Joseph Selling, an American moral theologian from Louvain. Another third of the bishops felt they had to reinterpret the pope's remarks. And a third of the world's bishops, as far as Selling could tell, accepted the pope's reasoning. (His batting average with the bishops—only .333—depressed him; Paul VI would never write another encyclical.)

John Paul II has chosen to push this teaching, and has even made his position on birth control a litmus test for any appointments to the episcopacy. Even so, the vast majority of Catholic couples, according to polls in the western world at least, have made a conscientious decision in this regard and dissented from the pope's position. Some conservative commentators charge that these couples are simply disobedient. Others disagree. They say this provides us with a good contemporary example of a papal teaching that has not been "received" by the people of God. In which case, some commentators say, this is not a "teaching" at all. A bell is no bell 'til you ring it. A song is no song 'til you sing it.

So when John Paul uses the term "reception," I'd like to think the pope has come to a sudden insight about the intent of Vatican II—to give the church back to the people. Which means that he (and everyone in the church) ought to value public opinion in the church.

THE CHURCH NEEDS US to be more vocal. We all love what happened at Vatican II. But if the church has dumbed the council down in the last thirty-five years, I maintain this is because we, the people of God, have not been vocal enough. We need to start doing what the fathers of the council did: we have to learn to *speak out*. Or, as theologian Monica Hellwig tells us, we have to be prophets. Until Dr. Hellwig pointed this out (see chapter XX . . .), I hadn't realized that the Old Testament prophets were all very ordinary people. So, it is possible that we may even have a call, through our baptism. Our teaching may rise to the level of prophecy.

Because of our baptism, we can speak out *prophetically* in the spirit of Paolo Freire who called on his people in Brazil and Latin America to wake up to what was killing them—in a process and a movement called "consciencization," a developing of consciousness, but consciousness that is understood to have the power to transform reality. For Freire, educators must be prophets in the biblical sense: prophets denounce what stinks to high heaven and they *announce* the good news.

Because of our baptism, we can speak out *charismatically*, in the spirit of Saint Catherine of Siena, who once walked all the way to Rome to give a severe lecture to a war mongering pope Gregory XI, who had slammed his political enemies, the entire city of Florence, with a papal interdict—which meant they were forbidden to celebrate Mass or receive the sacraments. Due to a shortage of priests, many communities in various parts of the world today, from Arizona to Oceania, are under a practical interdict, in this sense, that they cannot celebrate Mass or receive the sacraments.

Priest shortage? What priest shortage? cries the Vatican. It doesn't see any priest shortage. I quote a story from *The Tablet* of London: "According to the latest Catholic directory for Rome, there are more than five thousand priests currently working in the pope's diocese—nearly fifteen for each of the three hundred thirty-four parishes." In addition to those five thousand, according to *The Tablet,* there are eight hundred thirty-two priests on temporary loan from other dioceses, plus another three thousand one hundred belonging to religious orders. Another one hundred fifteen are priests who belong to the personal prelature, Opus Dei.

The Tablet reports that this is only the beginning of the story. If you add priest-students doing post-graduate study, and other priests who have no apparent job or ministry, the number of priests in Rome rises to more than fifteen thousand. This is not to mention the thousands of not-yet-ordained seminarians, many of whom are dressed in Roman collar and black suits and some even in cassocks. *The Tablet* concludes: "With such a visible presence of 'clerics' in their own backyard, is it any wonder that the pope and his aides have a difficult time understanding why so many people keep complaining about a lack of priests in the world?"

More than fifteen thousand priests in Rome, while many parishes around the world have none. Are you tempted, with Paolo Freire, to denounce what stinks to high heaven and announce the good news?

I SUSPECT YOU SEE what I am doing here. I am being mischievous, egging you on to be prophets. I'd like you to talk about how you can *speak out*. You may not feel that you are inspired enough, or competent enough—or dumb enough (as I have perhaps been) to speak out about the abominations in the church that stink to high heaven. But you *can* announce the Good News. You can also give voice to what *you want* to see the church—your church—become. This is a prophetic act. As teachers—what finer (and least appreciated) vocation is there in the church than "teacher?" As teachers, you can be, must be, will be, key people in your own communities—helping to make the church more democratic, more pluralistic, more free, more human, more humble in the face of history. And more joyful.

On January 6, 2001, John Paul II suggested in *Novo Millennio Adveniente*, perhaps the most surprising (and most far seeing) address of his papacy, that the whole church get involved in developing other "structures of participation." John Paul II mentioned priests councils and pastoral councils. Whether he realized it or not, he was clearly talking about a new era of free speech in the church, with lots of consultation all around.

I agree with John Paul II. The health of the church demands the participation of the whole church. We should be having not only priests councils and pastoral councils, but synods in every diocese (much like Cardinal Mahony has already launched in Los Angeles). These synods should start at the grass roots with a determined effort to bring in laymen and laywomen, not only folks who are already involved in various forms of church, but men and women from the various professions—law, medicine, social work, science, media, business, and academe, and just plain folks, too, soccer moms and dads, and their kids. I would even suggest that if the whole church is going to be involved, then Protestants and Orthodox ought to be represented, too. And a few Jews. And some Muslims.

The twenty-first century has to reverse the clericalism of the twentieth. History is already dictating this, as we see the number of priests dwindling down to a precious few. It is simply up to us to take this trend as one of the signs of the time, one of the ways that the Holy Spirit is guiding us toward a new, less churchy future.

I have always thrilled to Jesus' own mission statement, that he had come so that we might have life and have it more abundantly. I say it is up to us to help make this life happen, each of us in our own way, right now, during the waning years of the John Paul II papacy. This is the most important time in the history of the modern church since the end of Vatican II. It is a time when the church in general and the college of cardinals in particular should be thinking and talking about the kind of church we want to live in when the Holy Father passes on to his reward.

The whole church needs your input. You have a duty to speak out as loudly and as eloquently as you can, to give voice to your views on the most pressing problems that will face the next pope. And even before we have a new pope, you should tell the world what kind of man you think the college of cardinals should be looking for when it comes time for the next conclave.

I say this on the highest authority in the church, an ecumenical council, Vatican II:

> In virtue of its mission to enlighten the whole world with the message of the Gospel and to gather together in one Spirit all women and men of every nation, race and culture, the Church shows itself as a sign of that amity which renders possible sincere dialogue and strengthens it.(*Gaudium et Spes*, 92).

Such a mission requires in the first place that we foster within the church herself mutual esteem, reverence and harmony, through the full recognition of lawful diversity. Thus all who compose the one people of God, both pastors and the general faithful, can engage in dialogue with ever abounding fruitfulness. For the bonds which unite the faithful are mightier than anything dividing them. Hence, as good Pope John has suggested, let there be unity in what is necessary; freedom in what is unsettled, and charity in any case.

Let us take pains to pattern ourselves after the Gospel more exactly every day, and thus work as brothers and sisters in rendering service to the human family, in Christ Jesus called to be the family of God.

Reading List

The Actual Documents
Vatican Council II
  Austin Flannery, OP
Available as a revised translation in inclusive language. (Dublin: Dominican, 1996)

Summaries of the Actual Documents
Vatican II in Plain English
  Bill Huebsch
A three-volume set that includes *The Council, The Constitutions,* and *The Decrees and Declarations.* This work is unique because it offers a summary of all sixteen council documents in engaging sense lines. A timeline of church history and helpful bibliography are included in this compelling set. (Allen, TX: Thomas More, 1996)

General Works on the Council
The Church Emerging from Vatican II
  Dennis M. Doyle
This is a well-written and easy-to-read treatment of how the council affected the day-to-day life of the church. This book makes wide use of anecdotes and stories as a way of situating

the council in today's church. (Mystic, CT: Twenty-Third Publications, *1998)*

A Concise History of the Catholic Church
Thomas Bokenkotter
There is simply no better, more objective postconciliar history of the church than this one for readability and indexing. (New York: Doubleday (Image Books), 1990)

Council Daybooks
Edited by Floyd Anderson
For the most complete story of the council's proceedings from the opening speeches to the closing bell, read these three volumes. They can easily be browsed and have an extremely complete index if one is looking for something specific. They are out of print but available in used bookstores or on the *Destination Vatican II* CD-ROM. (Allen, TX: Thomas More, 1997)

Destination Vatican II CD/ROM
For use in a school or home computer, this is technology that touches the heart. An interactive format allows learners to tour St. Peter's Square, view actual council footage, and interview council participants. The original council documents (ed. Walter M. Abbott, S.J.), *Vatican Council II* by Xavier Rynne, and the *Council Daybooks,* plus Bill Huebsch's *Vatican II in Plain English* are included with full word search, print, and "hot text" capability. Available in PC and MAC formats. (Allen, TX: Thomas More, 1997)

The Faithful Revolution
A five-video, historical documentary on the Second Vatican Council, the church's "defining moment" of the second millennium. This video series includes a study guide, which

can be used in parish and school settings. Black line Masters are also available to supplement school and parish courses. (Allen, TX: Thomas More, 1997)

Guests in Their Own House: The Women of Vatican II
An honest and sometimes painful-to-read history of the women who were present for the council, much of it in their own words. The author, Carmel McEnroy has researched this book very well and it's an important link in understanding, in part, what Vatican II did not do. (New York: Crossroads, 1996)

History of Vatican II, Vols 1, 2 & 3
The first major and exhaustive history of the council. This work is essential to anyone who wants to fully understand the provenance of the various documents and conciliar activities. Edited by Giuseppe Alberigo and Joseph Komonchak. (Maryknoll, NY: Orbis and Leuven: Peeters, 1995 and 1996 respectively)

People of God at Prayer:
18 Services in the Spirit of Vatican II
The church is the people praying together. This book does the preparation for you by providing personal or communal prayers, each celebrating one of the chief outcomes of the council. Written by Bill Huebsch, it's in 8½ X 11 inch format for ease in making copies. (Mystic, CT: Twenty-Third Publications, 2000)

Praying with Pope John XXIII
Written by Bill Huebsch, this work will put you in touch with Pope John's spirituality and vision. It will become an invaluable prayer guide for you. (Winona, MN: St. Mary's Press, 1999)

Vatican Council II
Xavier Rynne

This is a detailed account of the proceedings of the council itself and is still the best for accuracy, style, and astute observation. This version is a condensed edition of Rynne's four volumes, one for each session of Vatican II. Available as a book (Maryknoll, NY: Orbis, 1999) or on *Destination Vatican II* CD-ROM (Allen, TX: Thomas More, 1997). You'll also find this in some used bookstores.